THE 6th (BORDER) BATTALION

THE KING'S OWN SCOTTISH BORDERERS
1939-1945

Captain J. R. P. BAGGALEY, M.C.

The Naval & Military Press Ltd

Published by

The Naval & Military Press Ltd
Unit 10 Ridgewood Industrial Park,
Uckfield, East Sussex,
TN22 5QE England

Tel: +44 (0) 1825 749494
Fax: +44 (0) 1825 765701

www.naval-military-press.com
www.military-genealogy.com

In reprinting in facsimile from the original, any imperfections are inevitably reproduced and the quality may fall short of modern type and cartographic standards.

TO THE MEN
OF THE INTELLIGENCE
AND SNIPER SECTIONS

FOREWORD

BY

LIEUTENANT-COLONEL C. W. P. RICHARDSON, D.S.O.

IT is most appropriate that this volume should come into print at approximately the same time as the 6th (Border) Battalion is disbanded as it cannot fail to do much to perpetuate the memory of the Unit.

To Captain J. R. P. Baggaley go the sincere thanks of the whole Battalion for his painstaking efforts in the production of this History, which seems to me to be remarkably accurate. Captain Baggaley joined the 6th K.O.S.B. when it was formed and was appointed Intelligence Officer in December, 1939, and retained this responsible appointment until his release in December, 1945. The care which he has devoted to this volume is altogether charactistic of his work as Intelligence Officer, which was rewarded at last, to the satisfaction of all ranks, with the award of the Military Cross.

One cannot say that the reading of a history of a battalion in war recaptures "happy memories," but it will at least recall the pride which we all feel in the Battalion's achievements, gratitude to those of our comrades who so gladly gave their lives for their King, Country and Battalion, and the remarkable spirit and comradeship which were a constant feature of all ranks of the 6th (Border) Battalion, The King's Own Scottish Borderers.

Captain J. R. P. BAGGALEY, M.C. (Author)

Captain Baggaley, who comes from Lincolnshire, joined the 6th K.O.S.B. on its formation, and served with it till his release on the 11th December, 1945.

He was made Intelligence Officer in December, 1939, and held this responsible post throughout.

His devotion to duty and personal gallantry played a marked part in the success of the Battalion during the Campaign.

PREFACE.

In the summer after the World War ended, when it became obvious that those who had fought together, shared together the dangers, humour and more pleasant parts of the war, would soon be scattered, the author conceived the idea of writing an account of the activities of the Battalion and dedicating it to comrades and friends in the Intelligence and Sniper Sections, who had cheerfully and efficiently carried out their exacting and skilled, if unobtrusive, tasks ; often unnoticed, but nevertheless making a significant contribution to the success of the Battalion.

It has been the intention to record the events, and reconstruct the situations as truly and as accurately as possible after so long a lapse of time, and to avoid misrepresentation and "purple patches." It may well be that there are some inaccuracies in minor details, since the Brigade Command Vehicle I. log was the principal document used, and many of the bare facts are amplified from the vivid memories of those who took part in the actions. It is only in minor details, however, in which these inaccuracies will be found.

Owing to the appointment of the author this account is largely written from the point of view of Battalion Headquarters, and this inevitably means that many interesting incidents occurring in the Rifle Companies, and many men whose deeds were more worthy of note than those mentioned have been omitted. But this story is in the nature of a personal account. The author is very conscious of these omissions but hopes that those who served in other parts of the Battalion will understand their necessity. Some of the details may seem too trivial to be included in this history, except perhaps to those actually concerned. But it was felt that the presentation of the details available would give to the reader the best means of estimation the authenticity of the story, and would best prevent the writer from giving an unfair picture of his own Unit or of a particular sub-Unit by comparison with others.

J.R.P.B.

November, 1945.

CONTENTS.

FOREWORD. By Lieut.-Colonel C. W. P. Richardson, D.S.O.

PREFACE.

Chapter.		Page.
I.	FORMATION AND TRAINING	11
II.	THE BREAK-OUT: ST. MAUVIEU AND GRAINVILLE-SUR-ODON	18
III.	THE BREAK-OUT: EVRECY	26
IV.	CAUMONT TO ESTRY	32
V.	LIBERATION	40
VI.	THE GHEEL BRIDGEHEAD	44
VII.	THE FIGHTING ROUND BEST	51
VIII.	TILBURG	55
IX.	RESTORING THE LINE OF THE MAAS	59
X.	BLERICK, AND THE WATCH ON THE MAAS	69
XI.	THE SIEGFRIED LINE	77
XII.	GOCH AND SCHLOSS KALBECK	84
XIII.	THE RHINE CROSSING	91
XIV.	THE CHASE THROUGH GERMANY	100
XV.	THE ELBE	106
XVI.	THE END	110
	EPILOGUE	113
	APPENDIX "A"—HONOURS AND AWARDS	114

LIST OF MAPS.

ST. MAUVIEU AND EVRECY	26
CAUMONT AND ESTRY	32
BEST AND TILBURG	55
DEURNE TO MEIJEL	69
THE SIEGFRIED LINE	84
THE RHINE CROSSING	91
UELZEN	100
THE ELBE	106

Lieut.-Colonel THE LORD NAPIER AND ETTRICK, D.L.

Commissioned in 1920, Lieut.-Colonel The Lord Napier and Ettrick assumed command of the 6th (Border) Battalion on the 2nd September, 1939, thus being responsible for the formation and initial training of the Unit.

Lord Napier and Ettrick was succeeded in command by Lieut.-Colonel Shillington on the 14th October, 1941.

CHAPTER I.

FORMATION AND TRAINING.

HISTORIES are most interesting when they deal with periods of crisis, and in the case of a battalion, the period of crisis is the period of fighting. The majority of this book, therefore, is devoted to an account of the parts played by the 6th (Border) Battalion K.O.S.B., in the campaign in North-West Europe, from June, 1944, to May, 1945—a part both strenuous and distinguished. That it was able to do so was due to the fact that it arrived on the shores of Normandy, a disciplined, fit and skilful Battalion, and a part of a well-trained Division as yet untried in battle. By way of introduction to the history of the campaign, this first chapter is devoted to giving a brief summary of the activities of the four and a half years prior to D-Day.

When the 250th Anniversary of the recruiting of the Regiment was celebrated in August, 1939, the 4th Battalion was at Dreghorn having its annual Territorial Camp, and was in process of dividing into the 4th and 6th Battalions. It had hoped to give to each Battalion a narrow territorial basis, but the camp had only been finished for three weeks when it was obvious that war was imminent and there was not sufficient time in which to organise the two Battalions on those lines. Key parties were summoned to Galashiels a fortnight before war was declared, and the 4th Battalion, consisting of those men who had enlisted before 1st March, 1939, was soon embodied and sent to Portobello. Men who had enlisted after that date were then called up and embodied on 1st September to form the 6th Battalion under command of Lieut.-Colonel the Hon. The Master of Napier. Major C. J. Ballantyne was Second-in-Command, and Lieutenant A. E. S. Jackson, who had been assisting Captain J. B. A. Hankey as Adjutant of the 4th Battalion, was made Adjutant of the 6th. Those Officers on the Reserve who had not attended the Territorial Camp in August, Captain R. B. Bennet, Captain Alistair Bannerman, Lieutenant R. J. Middlemas, Lieutenant J. W. Ogilvie, Lieutenant J. E. Sanderson, and Lieutenant Tommison arrived on that day. The Battalion was at once organised on the basis of Detachments and Companies. Captain Bennet, with Lieutenant Middlemas as his Second-in-Command, commanded " A " Company, which was drawn from Jedburgh, Kelso, Melrose, St. Boswells and Newcastleton. Captain Bannerman commanded " B " Company, the Hawick Company. " C " Company, drawn from Galashiels, was commanded by Lieutenant Sanderson, and Lieutenant Smith, with Lieutenant Ogilvie as Second-in-Command, commanded " D " Company, which consisted of detachments from Ayton, Duns and Chirnside. Headquarter's Company, under Lieutenant Tommison, was made up of men from most of the detachments, but principally from Galashiels and Selkirk, whence came the entire Signal Platoon under Second-Lieutenant W. T. Dundas.

During these early days, there was no time for anything but administration and equipping the Battalion. But by October, when the Battalion concentrated in Melrose, it was ready for basic training—drill, weapon, training and route marches. The Commanding Officer used to say, " If my Battalion can do nothing else, it will be able to march." And march we did. In those days, at Melrose, were laid the sound substantial foundations on which the edifice of battle achievement was built. It was a happy Battalion which in those carefree, enthusiastic days applied itself with that grand spirit of the Border's comradeship to the mysteries of a life comparatively strange to so many. How patient were the Commanding Officer, and the Adjutant, with the gaucheries of the inexperienced, and how much we all owed to those stalwarts, Regimental-Sergeant-Major Hope, Company-Quarter-masters' Hill, Telford, Smith, MacLachlan and Kirkpatrick, and Regimental-Quarter-Master-Sergeant Moffat.

Shortly before Christmas, the 15th Division, granted by His Majesty the King the honour of the title 15th (Scottish) Division, was scattered across Scotland from Edinburgh to Glasgow, and 44 Brigade, of which we were a part with the 8th Royal Scots and the 7th K.O.S.B. concentrated round the capital, with the 6th K.O.S.B. taking over the billets of the 4th K.O.S.B. at Portobello, and assuming the vague role of defenders of the Firth of Forth. No one who was with the Battalion at the time will forget the bitterly cold winter when the whole Battalion was billeted in the Marine Gardens, where each Company had a corner of that great hall and when, on wet days, Companies managed to do their training to the accompaniment of the pipers who used to practise their chanters for hours, sitting like snake charmers at one end of the hall. One of the pressing needs of the time was a complete black-out, so that after dark the big hall was closed up, and it was the duty of the Orderly Officer to go before breakfast to see that all windows and doors were wide open. The result was that, not long after breakfast, the fog in the hall was so thick that one end could hardly be seen from the other. But, by some miracle, the health of the Battalion remained good throughout the winter.

After four months at Portobello, the Battalion began a series of moves at short and regular intervals. First we marched to Galashiels where we shared Netherdale Mill with the 7th K.O.S.B. But we had not been there three weeks before the whole Division moved to

Wiltshire, and the 6th K.O.S.B. went to Marlborough and the surrounding villages, to enjoy three weeks on the Downs in that glorious spring of 1940. By this time some important changes had taken place. Major J. G. Shillington had come from France as Second-in-Command, and Major Ballantyne went to " B " Company. Captain Jackson had become Staff Captain at 44 Brigade and was succeeded by Captain Sanderson. Major Bennet and Captain Tommison were both medically unfit and " A " and Headquarters Companies were commanded by Captain Ogilvie and Captain Smith, while Captain T. L. Birley had " D " Company.

At comparatively short notice, the Second-in-Command went to arrange billets for the Battalion in Woking, and at an early hour towards the end of April we arrived in Woking. Those were the days of parachute scares, and the good citizens, who had not yet got up, were startled by the sound of an unknown language in the streets. Anxious figures, some with fire arms, began to appear behind the curtains. Whatever suspicions they may have had at first were quickly dispelled by the sound of the pipes and drums; and once we had offered our credentials, we were given an almost embarrassing welcome to the hearths and homes of Woking. We were not to be there long, but we were there long enough to feel the impact of Dunkirk and the defeat of France, and as it were, to get a second-hand impression of battle from the wrong end: for the railway lines through Woking were full of trains loaded with troops, particularly French and Belgian troops, who had got across to our shores.

Such were the circumstances when, after three weeks, we moved to Braintree. Soon we were ordered to take over the defences of Mersea Island. That was quite the shortest stay we had in any place. Arriving about mid-day one Friday, we received orders on Saturday night to return to Braintree, and on Sunday night we were back in our old billets under orders for the East. Lieutenant Sid Delahunt and the " Q " Branch had a hectic time completing size rolls before the whole Battalion went home on embarkation leave, to return only to find that the order had been postponed and meanwhile we were put under command of 45 Brigade and given the task of defending Clacton-on-Sea and the southern part of Frinton in the event of invasion. This proved to be a tiring task, for as the summer passed on and the threat of invasion increased, so did our alterness in the defences which became gradually more exciting on account of the bombing. From Clacton we had a grandstand view of many an aerial combat as the Battle of Britain developed. Perhaps the most spectacular was one Saturday afternoon towards the end of a cricket match against the 6th Royal Scots Fusiliers, when only a few runs were needed to win the game. Someone heard a droning and there in the sky, vying in that untidy skein so charactristic of the German lack of formation in those days, parallel to the coast and towards London, was a mass of aircraft. Well over a hundred were counted when suddenly, as if from nowhere, six Spitfires roared over our heads straight at them, bursting the loose formation asunder. Several enemy aircraft were shot down before the battle moved out of sight, one, suitably enough, burying itself in the Corporation rubbish dump.

The situation at the time was rather anomalous, as we were holding an area in the middle of 45 Brigade Sector, while the other two Battalions of 44 Brigade were holding Brigade Sector further South. We therefore changed places with the 10th Cameronians on our right and took over the defences of Brightlingsea and St. Osyth on the left of the 44th Brigade Sector. It was here that we received word of the "invasion scare." The Commanding Officer and the Adjutant had not returned from watching a demonstration of some anti-tank novelty, Major Shillington was away, and the Intelligence Officer was sitting in the Orderly Room when the Brigade Major rang up and said, " Code word, Cromwell. You know what that means, don't you ? " " I'll soon find out," replied a rather reticent Intelligence Officer, and rang off immediately, to get in touch with Major Ballantyne who was temporarily commanding the Battalion from his Company area. " I've just had code word Cromwell, sir ! " " What the ——— does that mean ? " " I think it means ' Stand to ' but I'll find out," replied the Intelligence Officer. At that moment the Home Guard Commander rang up, " I've just received the order to stand to . . . " " Thanks very much," interrupted the Intelligence Officer and triumphantly confirmed his suspicions to Major Ballantyne. At length, after a day or two, the stand down order was received, and we relaxed, wondering in those days of keen security quite what had been happening.

After spending October in Roman Way Camp at Colchester, we went into No 11 Corps reserve at Epping, with " D " Company guarding North Weald aerodrome, and the other Companies round the town. Here we spent a strenuous and very noisy winter—noisy because of the blitz on London, and strenuous because of the formation training which was being done. Strangely enough, the aerodrome was not bombed after we arrived, but Epping itself was bombed on several occasions, and a tragic incident occurred on the 19th November when a land mine hit the pleasure park at Theydon Bois where two Platoons of " A " Company were billeted. We lost some sixty men as a result, thirty of whom were killed. It would be ungrateful not to mention this disaster without remembering the splendid help given to us by the local Civil Defence Services and by the hospital.

During that winter in Epping, we started formation training which consisted of a Brigade or Divisional Exercise at least every

LIEUT.-COLONEL J. G. SHILLINGTON, D.S.O.

Lieut.-Colonel J. G. Shillington, who is a Northern Irishman, was commissioned in 1920. He assumed command of the 6th K.O.S.B. on the 14th July, 1941, and took the Battalion to Normandy.

Lieut.-Colonel Shillington was badly wounded at Evrecy on the 16th July, 1944.

month, and sometimes more frequently, and as the remainder of the Brigade was in the area of Clare and Long Melford, our exercises usually began a day before theirs and ended a day later. We must have attacked the River Lark by day or by night with tanks or without tanks, from all directions at least half a dozen times, and Icklingham Bridge and Foxearth will remain in the memory for many years to come. In addition to these exercises, we had a weekly practice of our operational role, and every Thursday morning used to attack the high ground overlooking Broxbourne and North Weald aerodromes, and limited our exploitation to Nazing cross-roads.

When the invasion season returned, we went back to the coast and took over the landward defences of Lowestoft, while the 8th Royal Scots and the 7th K.O.S.B. manned the beaches. Here the order of the day was digging by light and bombing by dark, punctuated by one or two big exercises, including "Bumper." Many changes took place in the Battalion during our stay there. Lieutenant-Colonel the Lord Napier and Ettrick left us and his place was taken by Lieutenant-Colonel Shillington who immediately set to work to get the Battalion up to establishment with as many Officers from regular battalions as possible. Major W. E. J. Waters took over "H.Q." Company from Captain Smith who went to "C" Company. Captain Sanderson went to "B" Company, with Captain J. B. B. Bromilow as his Second-in-Command, while Captain A. M. Sturrock, who had been Transport Officer, became Adjutant. Major J. D. A. S. Coke and Captain N. C. Rollo in turn commanded "A" Company, and Major W. F. R. Turner became Second-in-Command. Captain J. Wilson, M.M., became Quartermaster in place of Lieutenant Delahunt, who at the beginning of a mile race for all Officers, their corresponding Warrant Officers or Sergeants and their batmen, tripped up when tipped as the winner and damaged his ankle. The whole Battalion gradually became full to war establishment.

But this full state was not to last. The Division became a lower establishment division, and when, in October, we moved to the coastal area immediately south of Berwick, the discouraging process of drafting began and lasted all through the winter and next year until a few days before Christmas, 1942, when the Commanding Officer was able to announce that the Division was again a first line Division, that drafting would cease, and that 6 Guards Tank Brigade was part of the Division in place of 45 Brigade. Innumerable exercises were held in all parts of Northumberland. We defended or attacked the various river lines there, even the Tweed itself, marched and operated over the moors in the West, and went to Catterick for one or two exercises with the Guards; the seeds of that close liaison with them which was to bear fruit later were being sown. An equally fruitful co-operation with 178 Field Battery of 181 Field

Regiment Royal Artillery was also developed in these months of hard training, and we were beginning to appreciate what would be our role when at length the invasion would take place. We knew Northumberland thoroughly before we left it to move South, having been stationed near Berwick, then at Felton, and Whitley Bay, and finally in the area of Prudhoe and Bywell. Two further important changes took place while we were in Northumberland. When Major Turner went to command the 5th Battalion, his place was taken by Major C. W. P. Richardson, and Lieutenant J. W. A. Smith replaced Captain Wilson as Quartermaster.

In the summer of 1943, the 15th Scottish Division joined 8 Corps in Yorkshire, and the Battalion went to Boroughbridge to perfect training for the invasion. We now knew what role we would have to fill on the Continent, and during our stay there we completed training for it. Again the composition of the Division changed. 6 Guards Tank Brigade went south, and their place was taken by the 227th Brigade. The Corps had taken its final shape, and with the two full scale excercises, " Blackcock " and " Eagle," training was complete. After this intensive period, Lieutenant-General Sir Richard O'Connor ordered a ten-day holiday for everyone so that all should be fresh for the battle. Then began the process of water-proofing vehicles. A crisis nearly arose when it was discovered that Ford vehicles could not be waterproofed. The Division was equipped with Fords, and vehicles of various Units in the Division carried out a test near Leeds to prove this fact. This put the Technical Sergeant, Sergeant Bob Anderson, right on his mettle. He had always been very proud of his transport, and he was not going to be beaten no matter what high ranking R.E.M.E. Officers said. When the trail came, the vehicles of first one Unit and then of another were called down to the water, and one by one they drowned. Eventually, the six loaded vehicles of the 6th K.O.S.B. were called, and all but one went through with the greatest ease. It was a great triumph for Sergeant Anderson and no doubt he saved the country thousands of pounds, quite apart from preventing any delay in the invasion.

In April, 1944, when leave was stopped and censorship began, everyone was thoroughly aware that the consummation of all these years of training could not now be far away. We moved to Worthing which was packed with troops, completed waterproofing and made final adjustments. The team was ready. Major R. N. Gilbertson, seconded from the Royal Scots, commanded " A " Company ; Major C. J. Ballantyne commanded " B " Company ; Major R. W. Q. Going, " C " Company ; Major W. E. J. Waters, " D " Company ; Major J. D. Henson, " S.P." Company ; and Captain A. H. Elder commanded " H.Q. " Company. Major Henson was detailed to bring over the residue transport, and his Company was in fact commanded by Captain J. Dun.

While we were at Worthing, one noteworthy sporting event took place. The Battalion had always had a fine Rugby football side, creamed from the Border clubs—a team which only once during the war had been beaten, and that a long time ago by the 4th Battalion. Before leaving Yorkshire we had reached the final of the Northern Command Rugby Championship with the Welsh Guards, but there had not been time to play the match. Now both Units were on the South coast, and it was arranged that the final should be played there. So it came about that the final of the Northern Command Championship was played at Brighton in May, and the 6th K.O.S.B. won by 11 points to nil. Before many weeks were over this magnificent team was to be broken. Captain Dun, Sergeant Butler, Sergeant Gladstone, Private Carruthers and Private Crosier were killed, and Company Sergeant-Major Burrel, Sergeant Bryden, Corporal Cowe, Private Keddie and Private Richardson were all wounded.

CHAPTER II.

The Break-Out: St. Mauvieu and Grainville-sur-Odon.

EVERY day at Worthing an ever increasing number of aircraft of all descriptions swept over our heads to be followed soon after by rumblings from over the Channel as flight after flight kept up the preparation of the invasion coast. They gave a wonderful feeling of confidence in the operation to the army waiting below. Day after day those heartening armadas went out until the 6th June dawned, dull and rainy, but the convoys could just be seen, far away on the Channel horizon, and everyone knew that D-Day had come. A few days later, Major Richardson gathered up his maps and set off for France to reconnoitre the concentration area for the Battalion, and on the 14th June the Battalion embarked. The marching party, which sailed from Newhaven, landed at 1300 hours on the 15th June at Graye-sur-Mer and marched at once to the concentration area at St. Gabriel, on the road between Bayeux and Creully. The vehicle party, which sailed from Tilbury arrived later in the evening, but lay off shore, anchored near to *H.M.S. Rodney*, whose guns gave them a restless night. They landed during the following day.

War seemed very far distant in that quiet field at St. Gabriel, where the whole Battalion bivouaced along the hedges. There was little to do except go to Bayeux and buy those excellent cheeses, or write letters home. One of the most striking things of that first introduction to the battle area were those letters from home which were waiting for many of the vehicle party when they arrived in the concentration area. Two days later, Lieutenant-Colonel Shillington and the Company Commanders went on a surprise reconnaissance of the Escoville area across the River Orne, where the 6th Airborne Division had been fighting. But the contemplated relief did not take place and we again turned our thoughts to our original role. The Scottish Division had trained for these many months to break out of the bridgehead, and the area selected was that sector held by the 8th Canadian Brigade, about five miles West of Caen.

In those first experiences of battle, when one was all intent on the work in hand, and when the places through which one passed on the way forward to make reconnaissances of the ground over which the attack was to take place, hardly showed a trace of battle; even the shell-scarred villages immediately behind the forward line were accepted with scarcely a mental note. But after a few visits to the forward Companies, when the experience of being under fire had lost its early absorbtion, the full implications of that poignant scene in Bretteville began to be realised. Bretteville, named L'Orgueilleuse,

The Break-Out: St. Mauvieu and Grainville-sur-Odon

now a shattered desolation, deserted except for a few civilians who had dared to return, brave in their misery, and search the rubble that was their home for what things they could find and recover, their homes, their all smashed by the merciless guns. Who will forget that village, the reek of burning houses, the clinging, scented atmosphere of the ruined street in those bright summer days, the pathetic road sign, " Norrey. Merveille du XII Siecle. 2 K.M." : pathetic indeed, for its beautiful church was but a stump of defaced stone, the Calvary yet standing unshaken above the devastation ?

Soon the battle was to roll away from Bretteville, for on the 26th June, the 15th (S) Division was to break out of the Canadian lines and seize the high ground astride the road Caen-Caumont, and push on to the River Odon. The battle was to begin with 46 Brigade on the right and 44 Brigade on the left attacking the ridge of high ground stretching from Le Haut du Bosq to St. Mauvieu, thus seizing an O.P. line for the attack by 227 Brigade on Grainville-sur-Odon, Colleville and Le Valtru. The Lowland Brigade plan was for the 8th Royal Scots to take La Gaule and the 6th Royal Scots Fusiliers to take St. Mauvieu, while the 6th K.O.S.B. followed and mopped up behind them. The terrain was varied—open wold-like country being mottled by small fields surrounded by hedges whose dense growth concealed deep dry ditches which gave cover from the barrage to many a stubborn group of Panzer Grenadiers and Spandau teams.

The barrage of nine hundred guns opened at 0500 hours on the morning of the 26th June and soon afterwards the Battalion moved from its assembly area on the western edge of Bretteville, where the self-propelled 25 pounders of the Canadian Division were in action, to the railway west of Norrey station. At 0800 hours the leading Battalions left the start line on the forward edge of Norrey, carefully negotiating the standing corn which concealed a number of well dug enemy fox-holes. By 0830 hours, the 6th Royal Scots Fusiliers on the left were meeting strong opposition and were not yet across the River Muc, a stream which on the map looked as though it might have proved an hindrance, but which could scarcely be seen on the air photographs, and which in fact turned out to be the merest trickle. Twenty minutes later, however, they were in the outskirts of St. Mauvieu, and the Royal Scots on the right had reported " Ross Wood " clear enough for the 6th K.O.S.B. to move there. By 1000 hours, we moved up to the line of the River Muc, behind the 8th Royal Scots, and at the same time tanks of 31 Tank Brigade, who were working with the forward Battalions, had crossed the road Caen-Caumont, and reached a point about two hundred yards from Cheux. Further west, the 9th Cameronians, of 46 Brigade, had also crossed the road north of Le Haut du Bosq. Soon after, the Royal Scots reported that their forward troops were in La Gaule.

But although the leading battalions had gone thus far, there was much work to be done by the battalion behind them. One of the most striking features of the battle was the number of enemy who had survived the barrage, to reappear out of their slit trenches and engage us. They were not solitary snipers, but complete sections, each of which had to be stalked and eliminated. Lieutenant Jan Guettler, of the Norwegian forces, thoroughly enjoyed himself, using his excellent field-craft to hunt out these stubborn survivors of the 12th S.S. Panzer Division, and Lance-Corporal Ord, one of the snipers, carried out a brilliant solitary stalk and accounted for a Spandau nest which was worrying Battalion Headquarters from the left.

Prisoners began to come back, not only from our own local operations but also from the forward battalions. They were tough, determined fighters, some truculent, most of them proud, but strangely few refused to disclose their identity. Many were confident that it was only a matter of time before they would be rescued and the British Army pushed back into the sea! Several refused to have their wounds treated in the British Regimental Aid Post by the Medical Officer, Lieutenant W. M. Allan.

But the forward battalions were having a hard time, and enemy tanks were becoming troublesome, so that the Brigade Commander, Brigadier H. D. K. Money, D.S.O., became a little anxious about the security of the hard won O.P. line. "D" Company, commanded by Major Waters, was, therefore, sent to help the 8th Royal Scots at La Gaule. On the left the 6th Royal Scots Fusiliers had had a very hard battle for St. Mauvieu, and when a stiff counter attack was put in against them at about 1800 hours, by the 21st Panzer Grenadiers, the 6th K.O.S.B., less "D" Company, were ordered to help them. In a terrific downpour of rain, "A" Company on the right, under Major Gilbertson, took up positions south-east of the church; "C" Company came up on their left, and "B" Company, under Major Ballantyne, occupied the north-east corner of the village, thus completing the relief of the Fusiliers after their wearying day. It was while going round his Platoon positions at St. Mauvieu that Major Going, Commander of "C" Company, was killed by a sniper. Major Going had joined the Battalion in Yorkshire after being on the staff at the 15th Divisional Headquarters. He had immediately become a vital part of the Battalion, and with his endless good-humour and inexhaustible fun had quickly become popular with all. Sniping was continuous from the front and flanks of the position, and after heavy mortaring, a further attack developed from Marcelet at 2030 hours. During this counter-attack, Lieutenant G. E. R. Carey showed great gallantry in the handling of "C" Company, of which he had assumed command, and was awarded the M.C. for his action. Fighting continued until dark, when it died down, though there was

THE BREAK-OUT: ST. MAUVIEU AND GRAINVILLE-SUR-ODON 21

still a lot of sniping, and prisoners of the 26th Panzer Grenadier Regiment, captured by " C " Company, showed that a new formation was in the line against our flank. Once the position was stabilised again, we were relieved by the Herefords, of 43 Division, during the night, and just as dawn broke, the Battalion returned over those rain sodden fields past the orchard whence we had started, to a field near Le Mesnil Patry, where there was an opportunity for sleep and food.

During the 27th June, the general situation was that 46 Brigade was in the area of Le Haut du Bosq-Cheux, 227 Brigade had attacked through the leading Brigades and two Companies of the 2nd Gordon Highlanders were at Colleville, but the 10th Highland Light Infantry had been counter-attacked by tanks on their start line near Le Haut du Bosq, and in time had been surrounded. After a fierce battle, the tanks were beaten off and the 2nd Argyll and Sutherland Highlanders had seized the opportunity of dashing on to capture the bridge over the Odon beyond Tourville. On the following morning, the 6th K.O.S.B. took over the positions of the 10th Highland Light Infantry south of Cheux and west of the Grainville road. By now 46 Brigade had pushed a little further forward with the 7th Seaforth Highlanders at Le Valtru, the 9th Cameronians established at Grainville, but the 2nd Glasgow Highlanders were being heavily counter-attacked at Colville, and some tanks and infantry managed to infiltrate between them and Grainville. On our left, east of the road to Grainville, was a whole regiment of Churchills and numerous anti-tank guns, sited on the eastern fringe of Cheux. The approach of enemy tanks, therefore, was almost welcomed by the Units on the left, but hardly by Captain Rollo who was taking a combat team of " A " Company down the road to meet the Cameronians at Grainville. Fortunately, neither of the armoured combatants had taken the slightest notice of this party before it was recalled and returned safely. During the evening, " A " and " B " Companies pushed forward to the wood some four hundred yards south-west of our positions to give flank protection to the 8th Royal Scots who did a " partridge drive " towards Grainville Chateau on our right. The operation was carried out with little difficulty, but throughout the night there was heavy mortar fire on our positions, which was made worse by the tree-bursts so that casualties mounted.

At about 1000 hours on the 29th June, a tank engagement started on our left, and gradually the battle moved round on to the front of the Royal Scots between the Riveau de Salbey and Grainville Chateau. The enemy was bringing up his tanks against the Brigade position, and after a fierce fight, the Royal Scots had to come back a little, and the 6th Royal Scots Fusiliers were ordered forward to assist them. Fiercer and fiercer became the battle between the German tanks and the Scottish infantry, and at 1317 hours, Brigade reported that the position on the right was becoming dicffiult and that 49 Division, who were west of the Noyers road, must help. With the position rapidly becoming critical, Lieutenant-Colonel Shillington went forward to the headquarters of the Royal Scots to attend a most hazardous " O " Group and received orders from the Brigadier for a counter-attack on the Royal Scots positions should they be lost. Our own " O " Group, held soon after, was hardly less diverting, and was almost literally parted by an 88 mm. shell which whizzed close overhead. Very soon afterwards, Major Ballantyne was wounded by a mortar bomb. Major Ballantyne, T.D., was one of the few remaining Officers who had seen the Battalion form in 1939. For many years he had been a keen Territorial Officer, and his being wounded meant a loss to the Battalion not only of an experienced Officer, but also of a true Borderer. Captain M. W. Twogood assumed command of " B " Company. Although the position on the front of the two other Battalions was distinctly poor at 1845 hours, the counter-attack had spent itself for the night, and the 6th K.O.S.B. was ordered to move up to occupy positions south-west of the Chateau, " B " Company going ahead to recover the Chateau itself.

The Battalion moved up during the night and by dawn, " C " Company, now under the command of Captain Rollo, had dug in on the left of Noyers road, a few hundred yards forward and to the right of the Chateau. " B " Company was immediately round it and " D " Company in the standing corn on the left, while the Carrier Platoon sent a patrol to Grainville Station. In addition to our own anti-tank guns, which were deployed with the forward companies, a troop of 17 pounders from 97 Anti-Tank Regiment Royal Artillery was sited round the Chateau. No enemy tanks appeared that day, though movement was heard in the wood on " C " Company's right front, and there was always the suspicion that enemy infantry were lurking in the corn or using derelict tanks as observation posts. But apart from a little shelling and some sniping, it was a suspiciously quiet day—a lull between storms.

After the strong counter-attack of the previous day had been beaten off, the enemy gathered new forces with which to renew the attack. Sergeant A. Murray, who had been forward on patrol at about midnight, reported enemy in strength a short way down the road. A few minutes before 0130 hours on 1st July, the hoarse message came over the wireless from Captain Rollo, " Hello, Jig Able Baker," (this was our code sign), " Hello Jig Able Baker, there is a good deal of enemy movement in front of me. Over."

" Can you speak up ? I can hardly hear."
" I don't want to talk loudly. They are too close."
" Would you like a Defensive Fire task ? "
" Yes. D.F. 109."

The Break-Out: St. Mauvieu and Grainville-sur-Odon

In a commendably short time the gunners had brought down the first defensive fire task of the Battalion's war—D.F. 109, which was to become notorious before we left that place. Immediately, it was answered by a veritable tornado of shells and mortar bombs on Battalion Headquarters in the orchard beside the Chateau, and for the next half hour shells and bombs rained down on the area. An unlucky shell landed at the mouth of the trench occupied by Private E. Wilson and Private R. Starrit of the Intelligence Section. Corporal Dyson and Private Errington gallantly carried the other two across the orchard to the Regimental Aid Post through the shelling, but in vain, for they had both been killed. After this retaliation, the situation became quieter. Enemy patrols were thought to be in the area, but could not be located in the blackness of the night, and at 0415 hours we could report "All quiet." About a quarter to seven, "C" Company reported the sound of tanks in front of them, and a few minutes later the enemy began again to shell us severely. At 0700 hours, a heavy counter attack, with infantry and tanks, broke against "C" Company and the junction with the Tyneside Scottish, who were on the west side of the Noyers road. For some time the enemy tanks lay back picking off, one by one, our anti-tank guns from hull-down positions. But largely due to the skill of Captain Dudley Shaw, Royal Artillery, and Captain John Meredith, Royal Artillery, our Forward Observation Officers, and the accuracy of our gunners, the attack was held, and by 0950 hours had been beaten back. The action had been exciting enough while it lasted, and when the wireless sets in the Command Post became a little quieter, Padre A. W. Sawyer, who had been sitting in the trench giving moral support to the staff, turned to Captain R. H. MacDonald, the Adjutant, and said in a quiet voice, "Do you know, Mac, that for the last half hour, you've been saying, 'Hello, Big Able Jaker'?"

But the respite was only to last for an hour, and then six more tanks appeared on "C" Company's front, the forerunners of another and heavier attack. By now the enemy knew our positions, and the whole area, and particularly the two forward platoons of "C" Company were subjected to a most vicious and accurate shelling. For some time, No. 13 Platoon, under Lieutenant Guettler, and No. 14 Platoon, under Lieutenant Desmond Minchin, held their ground, with ever decreasing numbers, and then just before mid-day it was found that the unit on our right appeared to have withdrawn. Lieutenant-Colonel Shillington went up to see the situation for himself, amid the shells, and found that the decimated forward Platoons would certainly be completely wiped out if left in their present positions. Permission was therefore obtained to withdraw them about one hundred yards and Captain Rollo rallied the remnants round his Company Headquarters and No. 15 Platoon, which was in reserve. Company-Sergeant-Major Millar, who was firing the Company Headquarters Bren gun, was blown into the air when a shell exploded in the bank beneath him. Though very badly shaken by the blast, he walked out of the Regimental Aid Post as soon as he could was back with his Company in the forefront of the battle.

Meanwhile orders were received from Brigade to send two Platoons of " A " Company forward to reinforce " C " Company and make secure the junction with the unit on the right. Both the Colonel and Major Gilbertson felt that little success would follow this plan, and that the Company would certainly have very heavy casualties. A moment after the Company Commander had received his orders and was walking back to his Company, a salvo of mortar bombs fell in the orchard and he was severely wounded in many places. Major Gilbertson was a great loss to the Company and Battalion. He had joined us from the Royal Scots and immediately became one of his adopted regiment, respected and liked by all. When the Regimental Aid Post staff rushed out to pick him up, he told them to leave him and look after the many men who were coming back wounded from all directions. He was, however, sent back as soon as possible, but it was not until the end of the war that he recovered sufficiently enough to return to the Continent to command the 8th Royal Scots. It was some time before Lieutenant Woollcombe received the orders given to his Company Commander, and by the time he did the battle was dying down, and it was not necessary to commit the Company to such a hazardous action.

All through the day the battle raged—infantry and guns against tanks and guns. On that day the Battalion and the affiliated gunners became as never before, one entity in a comradeship cemented in successive actions. Often it was necessary to call for gunfire much nearer our own positions than even battle safety regulations allowed, but, such was the confidence of the infantry in the gunners, that never for a moment did they worry about where the shells would fall, and were prepared to accept the inevitable short, knowing full well that whatever requests were made to the gunners, they would be fulfilled as exactly as was humanly possible. It was always gratifying to know that, afterward, the men of the 178th Field Battery, Royal Artillery, were in the habit of talking about " our infantry " in exactly the same way as we spoke about " our gunners."

By three o'clock, " C " Company was very hard pressed, and had had tremendous casualties, but under the gallant leadership of Captain Rollo, the remains of the Company fought back with Brens, rifles and Piats. Not only were the riflemen becoming fewer and fewer, the anti-tank defence was gradually being eliminated. The enemy had begun his attack by shelling the guns with great accuracy, but the crews fought on until they too became casualties. For some time, the gun between Nos. 14 and 15 Platoons fought an action with the German tanks. Private Crozier and Private Brown were killed and Corporal Wallace wounded, but he kept the gun in action with Captain J. Elliot until unable to do so any more. Finally, only Captain Elliot was left with the gun which he fought single-handed until the enemy scored a direct hit in the gun-pit, blowing him out of the pit and wounding him in the arm. When he had recovered, finding his gun smashed, he came back from the position to meet Lieutenant-Colonel Shillington, who was also walking calmly about the battlefield, a great inspiration to his men in this difficult battle. After reporting the situation to the Colonel, with his usual cheerfulness and unconcern Captain Elliot then went off to the R.A.P.

But the position was becoming very difficult and the Commanding Officer had to report to Brigade that "the right hand position is partially knocked out. The anti-tank guns are knocked out and any help would be welcome." At about this time, Captain Shaw, Royal Artillery, who was sharing a dangerous observation post with the remains of the Intelligence Section in the roof of the Chateau, spotted nine or ten tanks in the wood on the right front of " C " Company. " D.F. 109 south west 400. Give us all you've got," he shouted back to the guns, and in almost no time there was the biggest crash on that wood we had yet heard. Apparently, the neighbouring Corps had also picked up the wireless message and they too had given a good deal, so that nearly every gun in the army must have fired on those tanks! About 1600 hrs. the enemy gave up the attack.

We had now an opportunity to assess our position. " C " Company had been reduced to less than a Platoon. " B " Company had had one Platoon obliterated very early in the day when it was caught in the open by gunfire. We had had about one hundred and forty casualties, including Lieutenant K. G. Buy, Lieutenant Minchin, Sergeant Butler and Sergeant J. Stoddart killed. We were able to retrieve our former forward defended localities and maintain them, supported by a weak Company from the 6th Royal Scots Fusiliers on the open right flank. The enemy did not again give us trouble, and a sweep by the tanks on the west of the Noyers road just before dusk showed that there were no enemy within five hundred yards of our positions.

There were three Mark IV tanks belonging to the 9th S.S. Panzer Division a few yards in front of " C " Company's forward defence lines—a tribute to the steadiness of the anti-tank gun crews—but how many tanks had been destroyed in the wood is not known. A few infantry of the 19th S.S. Panzer Grenadier Regiment, of the same division, were also found. But it was clear that the enemy had put his faith in a powerful tank attack to drive back our infantry. He probably expected to smash the British bridgehead, and it was largely due to the stubborn tenacity of the Battalion, and particularly of " C " Company, that the attempt failed.

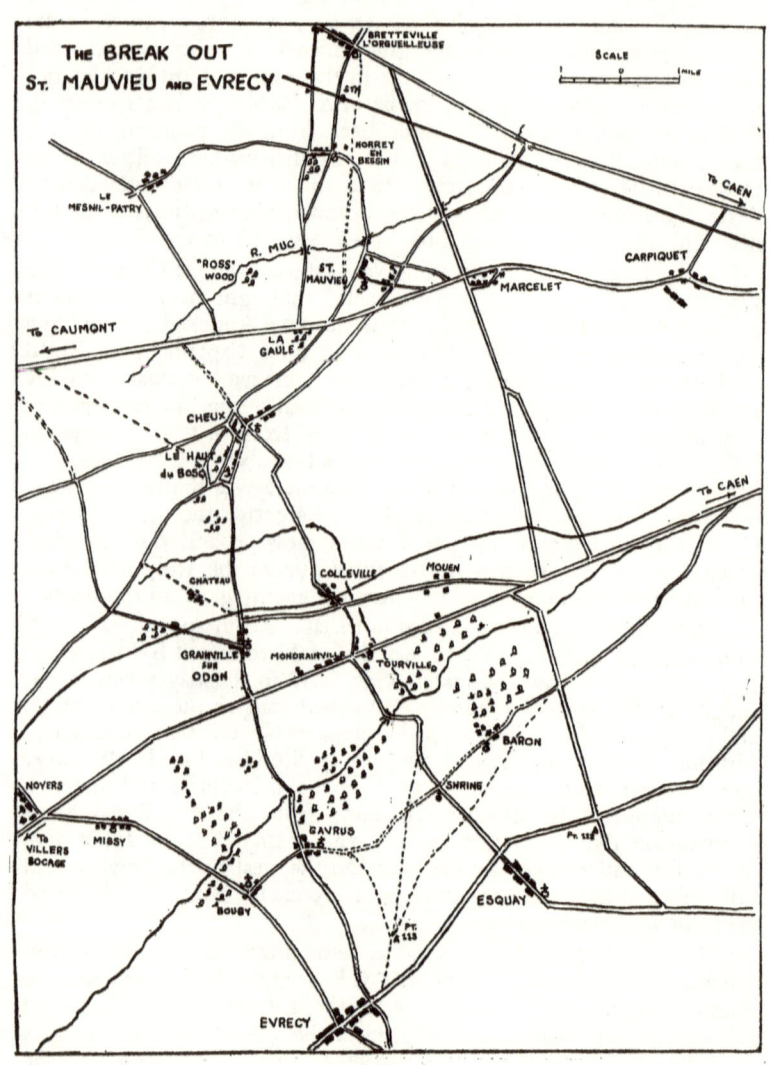

CHAPTER III.

THE BREAK-OUT: EVRECY.

IT was a weary Battalion which handed over to the East Lancashires the positions round Grainville Chateau, and marched out past " Dead Cow Corner " back to rest for a few days in a field near Secqueville-en-Bessin. But it was not for long. On the 7th July the Brigade moved into line again with the 6th Royal Scots Fusiliers at Baron, the 8th Royal Scots on their right, and the 6th K.O.S.B. north of the Odon at Mondrainville and the slope south of the village. The only road forward to the other two Battalions lay between " A " and " D " Companies and over the bridge across the Odon. The enemy had at any rate distant observation of this road, and in those dry July days the clouds of dust raised by any vehicle on the indifferent roads could be seen from a very great distance. Consequently, any vehicles using this particular road attracted on to the 6th K.O.S.B. a generous allotment of Moaning Minnies and other novelties. Mortaring and shelling were troublesome, but the place could not be compared with our last area in the line for hazard, though" B " Company, the left centre Company near the river, had several casualties from Minnies and phosphorous smoke bombs.

Probably the most trouble was caused by the cows, particularly after a wave of dubious humanity swept over the Brigade Headquarters and led to the inauguration of a Brigade Cow-pound. Captain Elder, the patient hero of many a piece of territory uncharted by the Battalion, was duly appointed Unit Cow Collecting Officer, and with Piper Gordon and a few other countrymen from Headquarters set off down the hill and up the other side of the valley to collect cows from the rather vaguely defined forward area, returning in due course with a large herd of miscellaneous beasts which were driven into the Battalion Collecting Point to await registration and backward transmission. It was not until after this party had returned that a definite trace of the forward defence lines was obtained, and to their horror they discovered that they had been rounding up cows well in No Man's Land. Whether or not the enemy mistook them for local farmers will never be known, but they carried out their task unmolested. Their chagrin can be imagined when shortly after they had discovered where they had been, a salvo of 88's landed in the middle of the yard where the cows had been collected, and killed or wounded most of them. However the expedition had not been in vain. A butcher was quickly found, and for the next few days the Battalion fed on fresh meat.

After only a few days we returned to the field at Secqueville to prepare for the next attack. By this time Caen had been captured after a heavy bombardment, and it became necessary to seize the ridge of high ground running south-west from Caen, between the rivers Orne and Odon. In this sector the British front line ran from about one mile south of Mondrainville to Baron inclusive, to Point 112 where the Durham Light Infantry were supposed to be established, thence back to Maltot where the enemy was making fierce and repeated efforts to push back the line.

The plan was for 227 Brigade to attack from the area of Point 112, along the axis Esquay-Evrecy, and after the 2nd Gordons had captured a piece of high ground west of Point 112 which dominated the road Esquay-Mondrainville, the 6th K.O.S.B. were to drive westwards from this road, starting with the shrine on the right, to the road Bougy-Evrecy. This attack was to be made at night with the aid of movement light. Once this ridge had been cleared, the 8th Royal Scots were to push westward along the valley of the Odon to capture Gavrus and Bougy, with the 6th Royal Scots Fusiliers clearing the north side to Missy. These two Battalions were to have the support of 153 Regt. Royal Armoured Corps. In their night attack, however, the 6th K.O.S.B. were only to move infantry and anti-tank guns in order to minimise noise.

This was the first attack in Normandy in which movement lights had been used, and for several nights before the operation the searchlights had lighted the greater part of the front in order to deceive the enemy. His defences in this part were facing north-west, covering the Odon, and the attack was designed to take them in the flank as much as possible. Our attack was to be in three phases. At 2230 hours on the 15th July, "A" Company on the right and "C" Company on the left were to capture the first half of the objective where a convenient track ran over the ridge from Gavrus to Esquay. This was known by the code word "Forth." "B" and "D" Companies were then to pass through—"B" Company to the right shoulder of the ridge overlooking Bougy, and "D" Company to Point 113. "A" Company were then to come up between these two Companies forward of the road Bougy-Evrecy, known as "Melrose," while "C" Company were to regroup in front of Battalion Headquarters on the left part of "A" Company's first objective. 227 Brigade were to conform on the left, and it was essential that the flanking companies should keep in contact.

The move to the forward assembly area had been timed to give the minimum delay there, in order to avoid casualties, but mortaring was very heavy and we suffered some casualties before the battle began. Battalion Headquarters, in particular, got its share of Minnies. This did not help communications which were already bad, and the difficulty was only overcome by the Signal Officer, Lieutenant I. H. Johnston, maintaining a relay wireless set near the start line. It was one of these occasions, so often repeated, when success was assured by the efficiency and steadfastness of the Signallers.

"A" Company, commanded by Major J. D. Henson, who, when Major Rollo was wounded a few days previously, had taken over the Company, having arrived from Maltot where he had been fighting with the Cameronians, and "C" Company, under Major Ogilvie, who had recovered from a cracked rib, reached "Forth" by 0030 hours on the 16th July. They had captured prisoners of the 991st Grenadier Regiment, but had met little ground opposition. Phase two began at about 0135 hours and was complete about an hour later, but contact had been lost on the left with the Gordons. Anti-tank guns went up as quickly as possible and reached their respective Companies safely, with the exception of those allotted to "D" Company. This convoy of four 17-pounders, and the Forward Observation Officer, Captain Meredith, Royal Artillery, guided by Lieutenant Murray, was unable to find the Company, and, on that very confusing hillside, lost the way and arrived in a village. So lost were they that Captain Meredith decided that the best thing to do was to bring down a D.F. task on Evrecy so as to give them an idea of where they were. They soon knew exactly where they were, as the shells landed around them! They also found that Evrecy was full of enemy tanks. They delayed no longer but hastily turned tail and eventually arrived at "D" Company.

Meanwhile, Captain Elder had gone up with a few Pioneers to site a headquarters on the ridge, which offered no better place than a slight cup near the road which had been noticed on the air photographs. Here they proceeded to dig. It took two days strenuous digging to make an adequate headquarters. Everyone dug furiously in that hard limestone in order to be well settled when daylight came. Tools had been brought forward in additional carriers allotted to each Company, and by dawn the Battalion was settled. The left flank was unsatisfactory owing to the loss of touch with 227 Brigade. The Brigadier had been killed and some of his staff wounded at the beginning of the battle, with a consequent delay in the later stages. This resulted in a gap being left open on the left of the K.O.S.B., and Evrecy, still in enemy hands, was a dangerous threat to our position. Moreover "D" Company was isolated and pinned by mortar and machine gun fire. At about 0715 hours, Colonel Shillington went out to find "D" Company but was not able to do so, and as he had been away from his Headquarters for some time, decided to return to find out the latest situation. At about 0800 hours he went out again. By this time the tanks had arrived on the ridge, and while he was out of his carrier talking to the Squadron

Commander, a mortar bomb struck the side of the tank wounding him severely. Private Tracey, the carrier driver, though wounded himself, managed to take the Commanding Officer to the Regimental Aid Post in his carrier and then return to Battalion Headquarters to report before going back himself. During the previous three years Colonel Shillington had trained the Battalion and brought it to its present state of efficiency, and his wounds, which prevented him from commanding us in future actions and seeing the successful consummation of his hard work, was a great blow. The Battalion was highly gratified when he was awarded the D.S.O.

In order to seal the gap between ourselves and 227 Brigade, " D " Company had to be withdrawn to the south-east side of the ridge overlooking the road Esquay-Evrecy. This readjustment was made under constant minor attacks. By the middle of the morning we had had several casualties due to mortaring and shelling in addition to the Commanding Officer. Major Ogilvie had been shot through the face while giving water to a wounded enemy quite early in the morning. The two Norwegian Officers serving with " B " and " C " Companies, Lieutenant N. Frafjord and Lieutenant J. Guettler, whose enthusiasm, bravery and skill were admired by everyone, had both been killed. Captain Jock Dun had gone out alone in his jeep and disappeared, to be found a day or two later having apparently met an enemy tank and been killed. Jock Dun, who commanded Support Company, had returned to the Battalion not many months before D-Day and immediately made himself a popular and prominent figure in the Battalion's life. He was one of the original Borderers, by now, unhappily, becoming few in number. Company Sergeant-Major Telford was badly wounded in the shoulder, but fought on to win the M.M.

On the right the battle was making good progress. The 8th Royal Scots had captured Gavrus at 0700 hours and Bougy by 1000 hours, but the enemy was reacting strongly with fire. Aircraft had been over the area in some force during the morning, and although thay had not caused any casualties by machine-gun fire, they had no doubt detected our positions. All Companies except " A " Company were engaged, and particularly Headquarters which was shelled consistently. Shelling and mortaring were particularly heavy in the middle of the afternoon, and the scout car was hit by an 88. It immediately burst into flame and several casualties were caused. At about the same time a shell hit the Regimental Aid Post, badly shaking the Medical Officer and his staff, already very fatigued by intensive work, and wounding the Medical Sergeant, Sergeant Turnbull.

Counter attacks now began to develop, first against the 8th Royal Scots, then from the direction of Evrecy against " A " and

"D" Companies. But at 2015 hours we could report, "Attack engaged successfully, and dispersed with heavy losses."

With the high ground captured, the plan now was for 59 Division to push forward on the right, and 53 (Welsh) Division to attack Evrecy that evening. From a start line in the middle of our positions, 158 Brigade began their attack at about 1900 hours. The attack went slowly, and before it had got to Evrecy a great cloud of smoke drifted across the battlefield from the north-east. Soon the whole area was blanketted with so dense a smoke that it was quite impossible to see further than two yards. The attack failed and was renewed on the following evening. But it had drawn more attention to our positions, and throughout the next morning we were subjected to very considerable fire. In the evening a counter attack of about company strength developed against "A" Company, but it is very probable that "A" Company had never been accurately located by the enemy. Previous to this, patrols had reported enemy surprisingly near to the Company's forward defence lines, but the number of the enemy was not appreciated until, at dawn that morning, Sergeant Cook and Private Maxwell brought back vivid information. They had been sent forward to a listening post, and when, in the morning mist, they had heard many voices they thought that our own troops had come forward and stood up, to be immediately captured. Sergeant Cook had the presence of mind to throw a grenade at once, and they escaped in the mist. On the occasion of this counter attack the enemy formed up to attack in full view of the Company, which was dug in on top of the hill, so that Major Henson was able to bring a great weight of shells on the Germans who had heavy casualties.

At nine o'clock the Welsh Division attacked again, and half an hour later 158 Brigade reported everything going according to plan. Prisoners began to pour back. We had had many from the 991st Grenadier Regiment when we had made the original attack but now so many came back that they were too much for even Sergeant Davy and Corporal Dyson, who was always happiest when he had a crowd fo prisoners to interrogate. The prisoners now were also from the 276th Infantry Division, and it appeared as though that division had given up the struggle. But later stages of the attack were not so satisfactory, and shortly after 2300 hours the forward Companies had to withdraw, having had all Officers made casualties. The commanding officer of the attacking battalion was badly wounded and was brought to the Regimental Aid Post by Company Sergeant-Major Lyall, Sergeant Henderson and Private McGowan, who went out in a carrier to find him. As the attacking unit withdrew, the enemy followed them, and the situation on our front became extremely confused. All through the remainder of that night small counter

LIEUT.-COLONEL C. W. P. RICHARDSON, D.S.O.

Also a Northern Irishman, Lieut.-Colonel Richardson was commissioned on the 30th August, 1924.

He assumed command of the 6th K.O.S.B. when Lieut-Colonel Shillington was wounded, and commanded the Battalion until its disbandment in February, 1946.

For his services in North West Europe, he was awarded the D.S.O. and Bar, Order of Leopold and Belgian Croix-de-Guerre.

attacks came in against us and were driven back, and about 0600 hours on the 18th July a rather bigger one was broken up by gunfire.

It was clear that the enemy had no intention of giving up Evrecy, and it was very probable that he had replaced the indifferent 276th Infantry Division by troops of sterner fighting qualities. He was developing the habit of holding a line with his poorer troops while armoured divisions, S.S. troops and the better Wehrmacht infantry were held for counter attacks. The Intelligence Officer of the 6th Royal Scots Fusiliers attempted to get behind the enemy lines and report on their movements by wireless, and was guided through " D " Company's position by Corporal Dyson and Private Errington. But he was unable to cross the road Esquay-Evrecy, and returned having found that the enemy was holding that line in strength. Mortaring and shelling, however, died down during the latter part of the night, and at 0940 hours, Lieutenant-Colonel Richardson, who had come up to take command of the Battalion after Lieutenant-Colonel Shillington had been wounded, reported that " the situation is extraordinarily quiet, and I think that something is going on. I am probing forward to the road Bougy-Evrecy." A large amount of equipment was found and a number of enemy dead. But the day remained quiet until about 1300 hours when heavy shelling began again round Battalion Headquarters.

It was, however, our last night in that wearying place. The 1st Highland Light Infantry began to relieve us after dark and everything went well until a German patrol appeared in " C " Company's area as the relief was in progress. This was engaged and driven off, but it very probably reported the relief, for the march back from the ridge was one of the worst experiences of the campaign. Battalion Headquarters, especially, suffered serious casualties. Sergeant Dempsey, the Signal Sergeant, was killed, and Company Sergeant-Major Lyall and many others wounded. Even our rest area was shelled. About 1700 hours on the following day, it was apparent that the enemy had got the range of the field in which we were, and a salvo, which killed the Mess Sergeant, Sergeant C. Dyson, and wounded Private Fuller and Private Spencer, decided the Commanding Officer to move the Battalion. It was a timely move, for when one of the Quartermaster's staff returned to the field on the following day, there was hardly a square yard of it which did not show a shell mark.

CHAPTER IV.

Caumont to Estry.

ONE of the most soothing experiences of the campaign was the move out of the devastated shell-torn Caen area, so full of painful associations, to the area west of Caumont. It was like going into a peaceful summer garden after a bleak and cheerless desert, when on the 23rd July the Battalion moved to Beziers, some four miles west of Caumont, to relieve a unit of the American 5th Infantry Division. We had moved back into the current of human life to an area little damaged by the war, and where the villagers were living their normal lives not many yards from our own positions. Some shelling there was, but not much, and the contrast with the place we had left was most restful. Beziers itself lay behind the forward positions occupied by the 8th Royal Scots and the 6th Royal Scots Fusiliers, but each battalion was responsible for patrolling certain areas in front. It was quickly found that the enemy were holding positions not far from our forward defence lines. Lieutenant Parmley, who took a patrol to La Vionniere, was fired at from several places during the night, but the enemy was not in the least aggressive.

The 15th Division had been moved across to the right of the Second Army preparatory to attacking south through Caumont, while the Americans attacked on the west. On the 26th July the American 5th Division began their attack, and on the 29th July, 44 Brigade took over Caumont from 227 Brigade, thus leaving them free to attack at dawn the following day. The plan was for the Division to attack along the axes of the two roads running southward out of Caumont, with 46 Brigade on the right and 227 Brigade on the left. 43 Division was to attack simultaneously on the left. For the operation, the 6th Guards' Tank Brigade were under command of the Scottish Division.

The attack began at 0655 hours, on 30th July, and resistance soon stiffened. By 1000 hours, the 2nd Argyll and Sutherland Highlanders, of 227 Brigade had reached La Londe after hard fighting. 46 Brigade on the right road were meeting even stiffer opposition. As the day wore on the possibility of the 6th K.O.S.B. being used to assist the 46th Brigade became evident, and Lieutenant-Colonel Richardson went forward to find the position on the 9th Cameronian's front, narrowly missing being "typhooned" while there. We were not, however, employed, but moved up close behind 46 Brigade to be ready for any eventuality. During the following day the leading Brigades made slow progress against

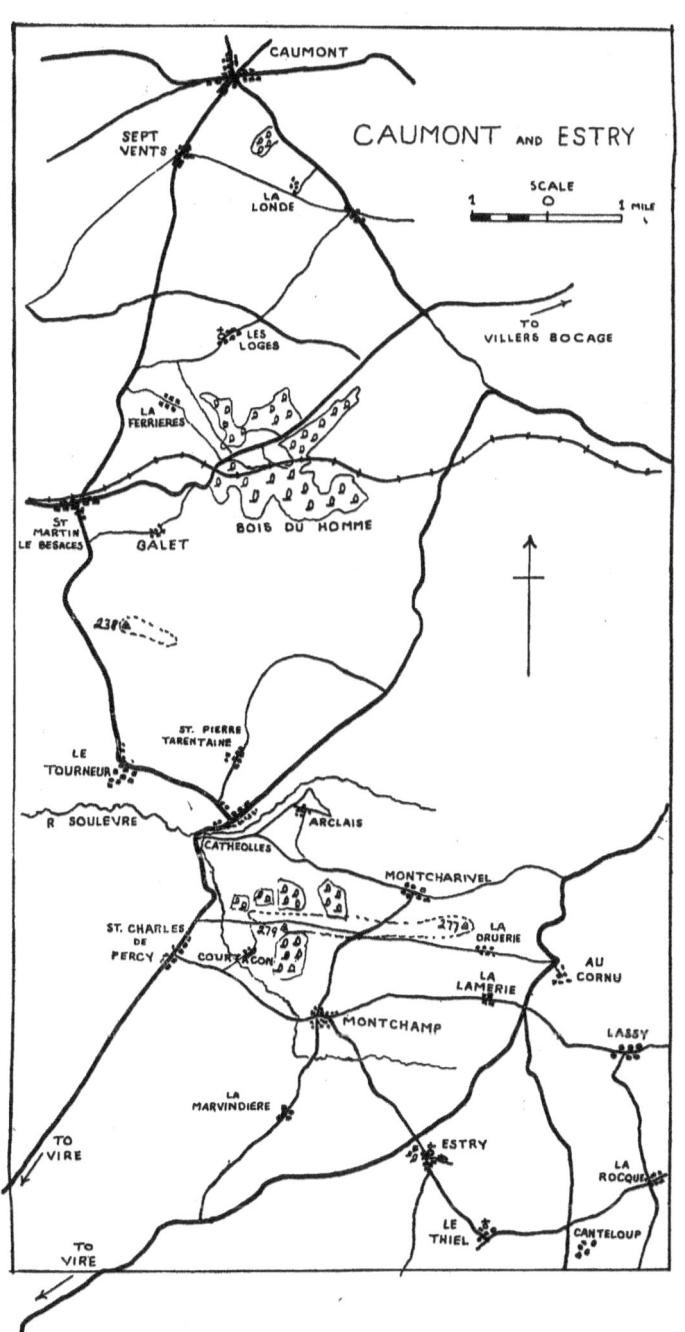

constant counter attacks, and the Reconnaissance Regiment, who were probing ahead, reported the crossings over the river south of the road from St. Martin des Besaces held, and enemy armour in the area.

The 11th Armoured Division on the right, and the Guards' Armoured Division in rear, were waiting to move through to Vire and Tinchbrai when opportunity arose. But at present the enemy showed no signs of cracking, but rather of strenghening his positions, and conditions were not yet suitable for an armoured thrust. Suddenly, the enemy did give, and the 9th Cameronians occupied St. Martin during the morning of the 31st July, but the high ground immediately east of St. Martin and astride the road St. Martin-Villers Bocage was strongly held and stopped the advance of 46 Brigade. Meanwhile the 8th Royal Scots with 4 Tank Grenadier Guards had " reacted," to use the current phrase, to a report of enemy armour on the high ground south-east of La Ferriere. On the morning of the 1st August the position was that part of the Guards' Armoured Division was on Point 238, south-east of St. Martin and south of 46 Brigade, being attacked by tanks of the 21st Panzer Division who had already attacked the 7th Seaforths at Galet: the 8th Royal Scots were south-east of La Ferriere on the right flank of 227 Brigade. A report was now received that fifty more tanks were moving into the battle area from the south, and thus the gap between the 46th Brigade and the 8th Royal Scots was a serious weakness in our line, and the 6th K.O.S.B. were ordered to attack in the late afternoon to fill this gap. So the situation arose for the K.O.S.B. to fight another battle on Minden Day, and the Borderers went into battle with roses in their hats just as their forebears of the Twenty-fifth of Foot had done in the eighteenth century. With " A " Company on the right under Major Rollo, " B " Company in the centre under Major Henson, and " D " Company on the left under Major Waters, the Battalion attacked up the hill from La Ferriere towards the road St. Martin-Villers Bocage. During some heavy mortaring, Major Henson was badly wounded and his Company was taken over by Captain Malcolm King, who had recently joined us from the Royal Scots Fusiliers. " A " Company went well until they got to within two hundred yards of the road when they were engaged by two tanks and a stiff action followed, but eventually the tanks were driven off and the objective taken. On the left, " D " Company captured some prisoners of the 125th Panzer Grenadier Regiment of 21 Panzer Division who said that there were four companies of infantry and four tanks behind the railway line running through the Bois du Homme. One prisoner gave the additional information that his regiment was deployed with one battalion up and two in reserve— presumably in the Bois du Homme. By half past seven, " A "

Company had captured 18 prisoners of the same regiment, all of whom said that, " a large number of enemy were in the wood south of the railway waiting to counter attack." As a result of this information, seven or eight regiments of artillery fired on the wood, which was also attacked by Typhoons. The counter attack did not take place. One of the unsolved mysteries of the war is the origin of a rumour to the effect that we had buried three hundred enemy dead after our attack. The truth is that we buried forty-one, but a suitable reply to the Corps Commander, who required details about the three hundred, presented some difficulty. We had, however, taken a number of prisoners, and it was gratifying to see four or five Panther tanks abandoned on our objective, some because they had been hit, but one for lack of petrol so far as could be seen.

The Guards' Armoured Division now continued the advance down the road from St. Martin to Catheolles, while the 15th Division pushed southwards from the Bois du Homme. 44 Brigade was put under the command of the Guards Armoured Division for the operation. On the 3rd August the Guards had taken Catheolles but were having continuous trouble from the east, and the 6th Royal Scots Fusiliers were ordered to attack a wood east of the village. Meanwhile, plans were made for the 8th Royal Scots and the 6th K.O.S.B. to attack from the positions of the 1st Welsh Guards along the ridge running eastwards between Catheolles and Courtacon. Those who took part in the reconnaissance for this operation will not speedily forget motoring along that road running south-west from Catheolles to the Welsh Guards positions, in full view of the enemy who did not let this impudence pass unnoticed. All the same, it is open to question whether the Commanding Officer expected to meet an untimely end by enemy action before he met it at the hands of the Intelligence Officer who was driving.

Early on the morning of the 4th August, with the 8th Royal Scots moving along the crest of the ridge and the 6th K.O.S.B. on the left, the attack began. The first obstacle was a steep, densely wooded cliff which presented no mean difficulty to the infantry who were carrying all their weapons, tools and bombs since no carrier could negotiate it. After the hill was climbed, fortunately without opposition, there still remained a long drive through the woods before the objective was reached. By about 0900 hours, however, it had been taken. We had no casualties and had captured twenty prisoners, including two Ukrainians from the 4th Ausbild Battalion of the 9th S.S. Panzer Division.

Meanwhile, the 1st Welch Guards were attacking Montchamp on the south side of the ridge, while on the north, the 6th Royal Scots Fusiliers were pushing eastwards on the north bank of the River Soulevre to Arclais. Soon after mid-day both these places had been reached and 44 Brigade reverted to the Scottish Division. Although it had not been a strongly contested operation, the Battalion was tired through physical exertions, but in the afternoon further orders were received to continue the advance through the 8th Royal Scots to the eastern end of the ridge to La Motte, near Druerie, while the 6th Royal Scots Fusiliers were to take Montcharivel. What opposition was likely to be met was not known, but certainly the enemy were fighting hard round Montchamp. All day counter attacks came in against the Guards who, at 2130 hours, reported that they were surrounded by Tiger tanks. Considering the importance of this hill feature, and the number of tanks in the area, it was appreciated that the operation would probably be contested and counter attacks made. It was, therefore, essential that Companies should get established as soon as possible and that anti-tank guns, F.O.O.'s carriers and the machinery of Headquarters should get in position without delay. The move of these vehicles presented a serious problem. The most direct track forward lay just over the enemy side of the ridge, beyond which Panthers and Tigers were known to be, so that the vehicles and particularly the troop of S.P. anti-tank guns of the 91st Anti-Tank Regiment would be easy targets. The alternative was the road through Montcharivel, and the use of that depended on the progress of the 6th Royal Scots Fusiliers. There was marked on the map a tortuous and most unpromising looking track between these two, but it did not look as though it would take the vehicles.

It was dark when the Battalion started to advance along the ridge which was lit by blazing buildings and haystacks, and it was not long before " D " Company on the right reported a tank just over the crest and asked for anti-tank guns. Soon afterwards Major Rollo reported that he had almost arrived, but that he could not get on to his objective because it was on fire. It was now becoming imperative that the guns should get forward and Battalion Headquarters established, but the 6th Royal Scots Fusiliers were not secure in Montcharivel. The greater part of Battalion Headquarters, including the scout car, the Battery Commander's half track and the other vehicles had not moved, but the Commanding Officer had established himself on the road Montchamp—Montcharivel in his carrier with a small tactical Headquarters consisting of two or three Intelligence, one or two Signallers, and Captain Shaw, Royal Artillery, in his carrier. To this little group, the troop of S.P. Anti-Tank guns had attached themselves. An attempt was first made to get forward across country, but that proved to be impossible, and was only greeted by a shower of mortars and Minnies. Then Private Errington went on his motor bicycle to Montcharivel to see what progress the 6th Royal Scots Fusiliers were making, to find himself almost immediately riding along a mined road. The only other possibility was the poor track in the middle. Down the hill the convoy went, and an S.P. gun went to explore the track which proved to be useless. But every movement brought an inevitable shower of bombs, and when the explorer had turned round to return he found his way blocked by a tree which had been blown down by the last salvo. Nothing was now left but to try the track on the right. So the convoy began to turn round in that narrow road to go back up the hill, when the Commanding Officer's carrier, "Tweed," stopped, straight across the road—with no petrol! It was hauled up the hill by an S.P. gun, and a small party set off to collect petrol from the 8th Royal Scots while the remainder of Headquarters could do nothing but sit down by the side of the road and hope. Eventually, in the dim light, a shadowy column of burdened figures began to appear. It was Corporal Dyson, and Privates Errington and Day bringing back jerricans of petrol. But still the vehicles could not get forward and Tac Headquarters eventually went up on foot, except for Private Errington who had his motor cycle. When the enemy had become quieter it was decided to bring up the whole Headquarters along the right hand track before dawn, and with the help of Private Errington and Private Day as guides, the vehicles got forward safely, hidden by a providential morning mist.

After the Lowland Brigade had completed its task, 227 Brigade passed through Montcharivel to the area of La Caverie, and the Reconnaissance Regiment patrolled forward towards Estry. Civilians said that there were four hundred infantry and fifteen tanks in Estry, and during the 5th August more Panthers were reported moving to Estry from La Marvindiere, a little to the west 227 Brigade attacked the village on the 6th August with the 2nd Gordons on the right, the 2nd Argyll & Sutherland Highlanders on the left, intending to pass the 10th Highland Light Infantry through to go on to Le Thiel. Heavy fighting, however, developed in the outskirts of Estry, and counter attacks were made against the 11th Armoured Division further west. Meanwhile, 46 Brigade, pushing towards Lassy, found opposition considerable and were withdrawn to the area La Caverie-La Lamerie, while 44 Brigade were ordered to take up defensive positions east of Montchamp and north of Estry. Further civilian reports confirmed that Le Thiel-Canteloup-La Roque were very firmly held with considerable Artillery support. There were said to be sixty Nebelwerfers in the area, and the Germans were confident that they could hold it.

As 227 Brigade were unable to make progress against Estry, the 44th Brigade was ordered to attack on the 8th August. The plan was to attack with two battalions supported by the 4th Grenadier Guards, who had some crocodiles under their command. The axis of the attack was the road from Montchamp to Estry, and this was the dividing line between the battalions—the 6th K.O.S.B. on ths right and the 6th Royal Scots Fusiliers on the left. Zero hour was at 1200 hours, and " D " Company on the right and " C " Company on the left, both supported by tanks and crocodiles, began to advance. The going was bad and the armour could not make progress in the narrow lanes. A large concentration of enemy was seen about eight hundred yards south-west of the village, which was engaged by the tanks when eventually they came up, thus enabling the leading Companies to cross the road from Estry to Vire at about 1300 hours. Here they were seriously engaged by enemy tanks in the village itself and were pinned by Tigers operating from the area of the church. The 144th S.P. Anti-Tank Battery was called forward to help, and " D " Company, in more open country, was able to make further progress, but owing to the inability of " C " Company to get into the strongly defended village was isolated on its objective in a position which became rapidly more difficult. During the afternoon " C " Company was able to edge forward a little after Company Sergeant-Major Millar, with great bravery, had stalked an enemy tank, hit it six or seven times with a Piat and destroyed it, winning the M.C. for his action. But by 1500 hours they were absolutely held up just short of their objective by both infantry and tanks. The Guards made an armoured attempt to clear the village, but met with no more success. Meanwhile, the 6th Royal Scots Fusiliers on the left were heavily counter attacked from the east and had to occupy the positions lately used by the 10th Highland Light Infantry. At 1715 hours an attack by infantry and tanks came in on D " " Company, and the situation became critical as they had both flanks open. In view of this, the Brigadier gave permission for them to withdraw to the positions occupied by 227 Brigade to avoid annihilation. By eight o'clock " C " and " D " Companies on the south side of the road were pinned by tanks in the orchard not many yards in front of them. But by 2115 hours the position had stabilised and become quieter. " A " Company relieved " D " Company, and " B " Company, which had had a Platoon almost obliterated by mortar fire on the way forward, came up behind " C " Company, and Battalion Headquarters was sited on their right.

The situation was by no means secure. The enemy was still holding positions in front and south-west of us, and even sharing the same hedge as " A " Company. A considerable quantity of mortar bombs was constantly falling in the Battalion area, and during one spasm Captain George Young, Support Company Commander, was killed, and Captain Allan Twogood, the Anti-tank Platoon Commander, was wounded. George Young had been with us for a long time and, as Transport Officer, had been responsible for waterproofing all the vehicles before the invasion. On the death of Captain

Dun he had taken over Support Company, where his expert knowledge of vehicles and mortars made him invaluable. With his cheerful carefree ability, everyone thought he was one of those who could never come to grief, and he was a great loss to his many friends. Counter attacks were now constantly being launched against us throughout the 9th August, and casualties mounted. Soon after nine o'clock in the evening a large number of enemy were seen forming up to attack the joint between the two battalions, but was held off by gunfire. The position was, however, by no means comfortable and the possibility of a counter attack by the 8th Royal Scots to restore our positions, in event of us being pushed back, was contemplated. By 2230 hours the enemy attack had definitely been broken, and an hour later Division reported a German withdrawal—the first of many reports from higher formation which tended to be a little exasperating to the troops who were very much in contact with an obstinate enemy. "D" Company was now able to relieve "C" Company, but, by a sad mischance, their commander, Major Waters, was killed while going round his Platoons. The last of the original Rifle Company Commanders who had come over from England had gone. Ever since "D" Company had reformed under Major Waters at Mickley, the Company had been his very life. No officer had spent himself more for his men than had "Minnie," and, by the time of his death, he had almost worked himself to a breakdown for them. It was a sad blow to his Company and Battalion.

The 10th August opened with another counter attack which was beaten off, but sniping increased and it was decided to do a sortie with tanks in the evening. This produced considerable mortaring, but sniping certainly diminished, and the remainder of the night was quiet. But in spite of the persistent intelligence reports, there was no slackening of the enemy's defence in front of us.

Early on the 11th August the Guards Armoured Division and the 9th Brigade of 3 Division attacked further west and southwest of Estry, an attack met by enemy tank reinforcements sent from the east of Estry. The usual nibbling counter attacks on our front continued, but on the whole the situation was quieter by day and by night. Between seven and eight o'clock on the following evening Division reported that there was a withdrawal on the front of the Guards Armoured Division and insisted that the enemy were going from our front too, and that we were in no circumstances to lose touch—an instruction which brought from Major Rollo the caustic comment that as he was at the moment engaged in a grenade battle at close range, it was quite unnecessary to send a patrol to find where the enemy were. An hour later we were again asked if we were in contact, and at that particular moment it was most difficult to hear wireless messages owing to the very heavy mortar and machine

C.S.M. A. MILLAR, M.C., M.M.

    C.S.M. Millar, who comes from Berwick-on-Tweed, enlisted on the 20th October, 1930. As C.S.M., "C" Company, he landed with the Battalion in Normandy.

    He was thrice wounded.

    C.S.M. Millar's personal bravery and leadership were beyond all praise, and his outstanding decorations were no more than merited.

CAUMONT TO ESTRY

gun fire. It was probably the enemy's last show of hate. The 8th Royal Scots relieved the 6th Royal Scots Fusiliers during the night, and on the 13th August, when they took over our front, all was quiet.

It had been a very costly week. We had had severe casualties on the first day, and the numbers steadily rose as time passed. The gallant Company Sergeant-Major Millar, M.M., had been wounded again, as had Company Sergeant-Major Falconer, and they were very weak Companies which came back out of the line. We had also lost two Second-in-Commands. For a few days Lieutenant-Colonel J. F. M. MacDonald was with us before going to the 1st Battalion. He was succeeded by Major Sir Edward Bradford, Bart., who left us on the 11th August to take command of the 9th Cameronians.

CHAPTER V.

Liberation.

At last we were given a much needed respite in which to rest and refit and make up our numbers. The day before we left Estry, Major J. Tinniswood arrived to take over " B " Company, bringing with him a goodly number of men from the Border Regiment; subsequently, he negotiated the posting of Captain J. Moffat who took over Support Company, and Lieutenant Mark Haslam. Other drafts came from the 50th Division, so that we began to regain numerical strength.

By this time the back of German resistance in France had been broken. The Americans, who had broken through at St. Lo, had pushed down to the River Loire and now were driving for Paris and the Seine on the south of the German Seventh Army, while the British Second Army was pressing that beaten force in the north and west. The First Canadian Army had reached Falaise and was closing the gap between themselves and the Americans through which the Germans were attempting to withdraw.

As the battle area contracted, the Scottish Division, which had done so much to break the seasoned enemy forces, now found itself " pinched out." After a night's rest, the Lowland Brigade moved eastwards to an area to the south-east of those hard-fought battlefields of St. Mauvieu and Point 113, and the Battalion was billeted in the small village of Maizet, three or four miles from Evrecy. What a change had taken place since we left the area a month before ! A dump of oil and petrol now spread itself lavishly over that same hillside where we had had to dig furiously in order to live, beside the road where so many enemy attacks had been broken by our guns there was now a large prisoner of war cage, containing hundreds of dejected German soldiers, and the country around was littered with equipment, guns and mortars—the relics of that strong defence against which so many British soldiers had lost their lives or had been wounded. We were able to see the enemy's fire power round Evrecy and realised against what we had been fighting.

From now, for the next few weeks, we were to pursue a comparatively peaceful course across France, to catch up with the battle again. Moving up the west side of the beautiful valley of the River Orne, we crossed the river at Thury-Harcourt to harbour for a few days in the tiny village of La Motte on one of its tributaries near Cesny-Bois-Halbout. Thence through the ruins of Falaise to Eraines, a few miles further east with no operational preoccupation. The sight of those pathetic citizens of Falaise, returning in silent despair to the ruins of their lovely town, left an indelible impression on the sympathies, which, even the continuous heaps of destroyed German vehicles and tanks on the road beyond, could not efface. It was indeed highly satisfactory to see so much enemy equipment destroyed, but one could not but wonder whether the innocent country folk had suffered in the destruction and was gratified to hear one and all say that the Royal Air Force had been terrible when they attacked, but had been very careful to hit only the German columns.

On we went, through Le Neuburg, until on the 27th August, we stopped a few miles west of Louviers. The 227th Brigade had relieved the Americans there on the previous day, and the town might have been a south coast holiday resort in peace time. Major E. Remington-Hobbs, the new Second-in-Command who had joined us a few days previously, returned from a visit to Louviers in the afternoon with his carrier full of fruit, making the remark that he had opened the liberation season by being hit on the nose with a cucumber! Steel helmets seemed strangely inappropriate when the Commanding Officer went to make a reconnaissance of the Seine at Portjoie, his progress being steadily embarrassed by pretty smiling girls insisting on offering a continental welcome and making the conventional demand, "Cigarette pour papa."

The Reconnaissance Regiment were manning posts along the River Seine and one troop had crossed at Portjoie to find no enemy, though civilians said that there were ten S.S. troops in Herqueville, opposite to Portjoie. These enemy could not be found, though fire was opened later in the evening. An extraordinary air of nonchalance pervaded the place, and a handful of Germans were eventually sighted fishing on the Ile du Bac, a short way up the river. The Brigade crossed during the night. The 6th Royal Scots Fusiliers crossed at about 0030 hours on the 28th August, and one of their assault boats was hit by machine gun bullets while crossing. The 8th Royal Scots followed and the 6th K.O.S.B. crossed in assault boats at about 0600 hours, climbing the steep cliff to the Reynaud estate and pushing on with no casualties. There was some slight shelling and a few enemy could be seen withdrawing in the distance from Fretteville, but there was no resistance. It was difficult to realise that the enemy had given up this great river barrier which could have been so difficult to assault against determined opposition, but it was clear that there were no enemy in the area, so for the sake of comfort, we withdrew to spend the night on the estate. One tragedy, however, happened to spoil the day. A storm boat bringing across Company Quartermaster-Sergeant McMinn, Sergeant Crawford and five other members of the Battalion sank as it reached the east bank, and all were drowned.

On the following day the Brigade moved in an advance to contact formation for eight or ten miles beyond the river. The 6th K.O.S.B. was the leading battalion, with "B" Company as advanced guard. Our objective was the village of Houville which was thought to contain enemy. On reaching the outskirts of the village, while Sergeant Telfer's Platoon was held up by an accident, Captain Shaw, impatient at the delay, raced past in his carrier and made good his claim to the capture of the village. A short time afterwards a car containing two German staff officers, who did not seem to know what was happening, came down the road straight for the cross-roads which "B" Company was holding and were immediately impounded. No other resistance was met, but the local Maquis insisted that there were enemy lurking in the neighbouring woods. This information led to a big wood-clearing operation in the Foret de Bacqueville which involved the whole Brigade. After great exertions in fighting its way through the undergrowth, the Brigade eventually reached the other side, having found nothing. So the Battalion returned to Houville to discover that the cooks had captured six soldiers behind a haystack a few yards from one of the positions.

After a few days there, during which we had an inter-Company drill competition, and Battalion Headquarters enjoyed the hospitality of Mr. and Mme Bricout, who gave us enough geese to make a very good dinner for the whole Company, the advance was continued through Le Fouras, Hadancourt, across the bleak fields over which thousands in the Great War had fallen to gain a few yards, through St. Pol and Bethune. Information was now received that there were enemy in the area of the River Lys at Moorsele, and the Brigade was ordered to advance to contact through Lille to Roulers. The 6th K.O.S.B. were again advanced guard. It was reported that the road was clear as far as Menin, but that enemy were likely to be met after that. The liberation season had indeed opened at Louviers, and had been celebrated during the whole journey from the Seine, but now, as contact with the enemy got nearer and fresh battles approached, it became more and more hectic, reaching a climax in Haluin. There, the good citizens had just realised that they were again free and everyone was wearing festive dress. The streets were lined with national flags, and into every carrier, jeep or troop carrying vehicle which passed, fruit, cakes, wine, and flowers were heaped by grateful and enthusiastic people, to the embarrassment of many and especially to Brigadier Cockburn's plan. The column stopped on finding that the bridge over the Lys between Haluin and Menin had been blown, with the result that every vehicle was mobbed, and even the Adjutant was constrained to leave his wireless and go back along the column on a motor bicycle in an attempt to preserve an operational atmosphere. It was only when shots began to be exchanged across the river that the streets began to clear.

Our advance was held up for the moment, but the 46th Brigade on the right had found a bridge a few miles further east at Lauwe, and 44 Brigade was ordered to take over the bridgehead. Before 2200 hours on the 6th September, all our Companies were over and dug in, and " A " Company pushed forward to the northern outskirts of Wevelghem without trouble, but the enemy were certainly in the area ; a certain amount of transport was heard at Moorsele and shots were exchanged. Further to the right the other two Battalions of the Brigade had found some enemy at Courtrai, but soon dealt with them.

From Lauwe, the Battalion moved on through Courtrai to Zulte. This was one of the occcasions when the Second-in-Command could go ahead of the Battalion and choose billets ready for them. We arrived a little previously, perhaps, and when Major Remington-Hobbs was eventually tracked, he was discovered lying in a steaming hot bath, smoking a large cigar, with a glass of brandy beside him ! Billets had, however, been excellently chosen and soon Captain MacDonald was installed in the office of the manager of the Anglo-Belgian Brewery, blissfully seated amid cases of very good beer. Before leaving Zulte we had time to play against an ardent village football team, and play Retreat in the square—a ceremony which was always popular. From there we went to Zemst, a couple of miles south-west of Malines, where the arrival of Scottish troops was gracefully greeted by a recital of Scottish tunes on the famous carillon. It was unfortunate that opportunity of seeing more of that gem among Flemish towns was not available, but our spell of liberation was at an end, and more serious matters lay ahead.

CHAPTER VI.

The Gheel Bridgehead.

BRUSSELS had been officially entered by the Guards' Armoured Division on the 3rd September; on the 4th Antwerp, and on the 5th Louvain had been captured, and on the 8th the British Second Army had crossed the Albert Canal. But resistance was stiffening considerably in the area of this and of the Meuse-Escaut Canal when, on the 12th September, the 6th K.O.S.B. took over the positions of the 9th Durham Light Infantry of the 50th Division, in the villages of Laar and Winkelom, about a mile south-east of Gheel, with the 8th Royal Scots on the left. The volume of mortar and gun fire was reminiscent of the hard days round Evrecy and Estry. This was only to be expected, as the moors south of Turnhout were used by the Germans as an artillery range for the training school near that town. The crossing over the Albert Canal was constantly under fire, and it was while coming forward with the Company Commanders to get orders for the relief from Lieutenant-Colonel Richardson that the Signal Officer, Lieutenant I. H. Johnston, was killed. Ian Johnston had served with the Battalion since 1940, and in his various capacities as Platoon Commander, Messing Officer, and finally Signal Officer, he had always served the Battalion unselfishly and efficiently, and had earned the affection of all.

Apart from the occasional burst of shelling, the night was fairly quiet, the major excitement being caused by a lunatic who was caught wandering round the Battalion area setting fire to stacks. But there was a good deal of tension in the air, and a patrol of the 46th Brigade farther west caught prisoners of the 723rd Grenadier Regiment who said that their Battalion was on the west side of Gheel, about two hundred and fifty strong. During the night the 8th Royal Scots found that Gheel itself was not held and reoccupied it. Civilians said that two hundred enemy had withdrawn during the earlier part of the night. At the same time, 227 Brigade was moving up on the right and they reported that there were approximately seven officers and two hundred other ranks on the Escaut Canal in front of them, of whom the other ranks wished to surrender but the officers did not.

During the latter part of the morning of the 13th September, the 8th Royal Scots closed up to the Escaut Canal, astride the road from Gheel to Turnhout, and found that the bridge at the small village of Aart had been destroyed. The 6th K.O.S.B. moved up along the road from Gheel to Rethy to the area of Bratze, to be held up by a road block manned by infantry with a gun just short of the canal. "C" Company, now commanded by Major Stavert, cleared this by about 2000 hours and left detachments to guard the canal. About 2300 hours a patrol worked its way to the bank of the canal and found that the main road bridge had been demolished but that there was a small bridge across the partially destroyed lock gates which might be usable. It was hoped that with little trouble the tanks of the Sharpshooters might get across and the advance continued. "A" Company was therefore ordered to seize a bridgehead here. By 0200 hours on the 14th September, "A" Company had moved to the canal bank and had come under considerable mortar and machine gun fire. It was a dark night, and once this fire had died down a little, Lieutenant Lountain went across the bridge, and finding no enemy in the immediate neighbourhood of the far end of the lock, returned to report. Sergeant McQueen then began to take his Platoon over, but no sooner had the leading section crossed and begun to dig than they were engaged by two 20mm. guns sited about twenty yards half left and half right of the lock, and by riflemen some twenty five yards beyond. At the same time intense mortar fire was opened on the remainder of the Platoon, while guns firing along the canal made it impossible for more to cross. At 0250 hours we had to report to Brigade that "the passage is being hotly contested. The bridge is under fire of 88mm., 20mm. and machine guns. The Company has had casualties, including the Company Commander. The bridge will definitely not take tanks and possibly not carriers." We still had a section across, and in the hope that use might still be made of the bridge, Brigade ordered it to stay and engineers to make a technical report. This was done during the remaining part of the night, and the sappers reported that the bridge was of no use.

At 0745 hours we had to report, "situation virtually unaltered. A few friends still over canal but most of Company still this side. Considerable enemy opposition of all kinds. Two companies at present clearing woods on this side of the river." We had lost a section. Sergeant McQueen, Sergeant Pearson and Private Dunn were taken prisoners for certain, and weeks later information was received from 30 Corps that a party of British prisoners of war had managed to pass a list of their names to a Belgian civilian, and this list included these names. Furthermore, we had lost Major Rollo, who had been badly wounded in the legs and had died soon after reaching the Regimental Aid Post. An Officer of great courage and skill, he had won the M.C. for his gallantry in the early battle round Grainville Chateau, and throughout the campaign had shown himself a first class soldier and leader. When the stretcher bearers insisted on carrying him back to the Regimental Aid Post, his consideration was always for them, and he took command of the party so that they should be able to rest periodically so long as he remained conscious—a final exemplification of his character.

Meanwhile, the 8th Royal Scots had crossed the canal at Aart and were busy clearing the village against stiffening opposition, and they were achieving some success which had been denied to us. In fact, our position was becoming precarious on account of floods. At 1000 hours we reported that we should probably have to evacuate the forward positions. All the time the heavy mortaring continued and " C " Company's " O " group was virtually wiped out by an unlucky bomb. It was clear that the enemy intended to prevent us from gaining a foothold over the canal. Heavy counter attacks began to develop against the Royal Scots. The site of their crossing was accurately and incessantly shelled so that the sappers strove against incredible difficulties to build a bridge, and at 1135 hours we had to withdraw from the canal bank as our position was under about three feet of water.

Throughout the day attacks came in against the Royal Scots, and during the night the enemy infiltrated into the village causing some damage and consternation, so that at 0745 hours the position there was becoming critical. The 6th Royal Scots Fusiliers were then ordered to go across, followed by the 6th K.O.S.B. It was not until after 1800 hours that we actually began to cross, and by that time the 8th Royal Scots had been reduced to about two Companies. The 6th Royal Scots Fusiliers had pushed their leading Company to the road junction at the north end of the village and had beaten off two counter attacks, killing or capturing a large number of the Hermann Goering Regiment. Our role was to expand the bridgehead westwards and northwards. By 2000 hours, " D " Company, under the command of Major Edward Coke, and " A " Company, under Captain Woolcombe, were across, and " B " Company under Major Tinniswood was crossing, but we could not get our first objectives as the Fusiliers had been counter attacked off the start line and the battle was in hectic progress. There was a strange irony in the message received during the battle notifying us of an allotment of the Mobile Bath on the next day !

During the night the Commanding Officer went across to co-ordinate the plan with the other two Commanding Officers, and in the early hours established a small tactical Headquarters, consisting of the Intelligence Officer, Lance-Corporal Maddocks and Private Thompson, with an 18 set, and Captain Meredith, Royal Artillery, who managed to get the Forward Observation Officer's carrier and team across. It had been planned to break out of the bridgehead at 0800 hours, but shortly before that time a heavy counter attack was launched against " D " Company at the road junction and " A " Company on their left, which made it impossible. After an hour's fighting the counter attack began to die down, but Major Coke considered it was not possible to launch our attack for some time, and the Commanding Officer reported to Brigade that " the situation on this side is such as to make the carrying out of the plan impossible at present. There is heavy shelling and we are ringed about by riflemen at close range." No. 18 Platoon, under Lieutenant Parmley, had occupied a house at the road junction slightly in front of the Royal Scots Fusiliers' positions, but the pincer attack by the enemy against this position had forced them back to a position just south of the road junction. All the time that the Battalion remained in Aart, the enemy made every effort to smash this point of the bridgehead. Some weeks later, when we found ourselves in Tilburg, we were told by civilians that about this time the Hermann Goering Regiment had come through Tilburg bragging that a few Scottish troops had crossed the Escaut Canal and that they were just going down to drive them back. But in spite of many attempts to do so, it was the Hermann Goering Regiment who went back, very depleted and much less cocky. Turnhout, some eighteen miles north of Aart, became a collecting centre from which all the troops arriving there from the west were put into formations and sent against us. At 1140 hours in the morning a lorry load of infantry came down the road and debussed under the quick eyes of Lieutenant Duquenoy, Royal Artillery.

It was clear that these constant counter attacks would give excellent targets for snipers, quite apart from the enemy snipers who were operating on the flank, so Corporal Thompson and Private Dawson were attached to " B " Company who were facing eastwards on " D " Company's right, and Privates Stewart and Brady to " A " Company. They had several opportunities of using their skill during the day. Then about 1600 hours a further anxiety for the Command and Staff appeared when the Intelligence Officer happened to look at the canal and notice that there had been a considerable rise in the water level. Not wishing to cause unnecessary alarm, he called Captain Shaw who verified the fact, and soon afterwards the Royal Scots Fusiliers, who were holding the south east side of Aart between the Canal and " B " Company, reported that their positions were becoming flooded. If the water continued to rise, the position of the Companies, who were slightly lower than the banks, would become very difficult and perhaps untenable. It was possible, however, for Higher Formation to arrange for aircraft to attack the sluices lower down the canal and the water did not rise much more.

It was the intention to withdraw the Royal Scots during the night, but again the enemy launched a counter attack of about battalion strength against " B " and " D " Companies, and the Royal Scots Fusiliers on the right also reported movement in front of them. This developed into a big attack along the whole east flank of the bridgehead, but the infantry were able to hold off the leading attackers while the gunners brought down Defensive Fire Task 6894 on the rear elements. This task was to be used so frequently during the following days that it was to become as famous as D.F. 109 was at Grainville. But at this time 30 Corps were making their long thrust towards Arnhem and the administration situation was such that we had to be very sparing in the expenditure of shells which were being brought by air. In fact, they could only be used in event of counter attacks.

By 2100 hours we could report, " counter attack stabilised but hot while it lasted," but as a result of the uncertain situation the three Commanding Officers agreed that it would be inadvisable to attempt this withdrawal during the night, and sent back the message which caused some amusement at Brigade Headquarters, " All the Sunrays consider the operation of the 8th Royal Scots most unwise tonight." For although the enemy had been beaten off from the east, they were moving round to the west. It did not take long, however, for the gunners to detect them, and their progress was followed by an " Uncle " target with terrific effect. By 2140 hours the situation was definitely stabilised and the enemy withdrew, but throughout the night small probing attacks continued.

One position remained to be cleared. During the big attack on the eastern flank, the enemy had occupied the foremost house in " B " Company's area. This was the house chosen by Corporal Thompson and Private Dawson as their sniper's hide, and from its roof they had done good work all through the day. But in the heat of battle, the men occupying it omitted to warn the snipers that they were moving out into the trenches just behind, and it was with some surprise that the two snipers heard German voices below them. There they remained during the night. In the early morning No. 15 Platoon, commanded by Corporal Francis after Sergeant Floyd became a casualty, attacked to regain this house, not knowing that the snipers were upstairs above the Germans. A sharp engagement ensued in which the snipers joined, firing on any German who appeared in the back of the house, and then Corporal Francis began to fire at it with a Piat. This was too much, and the attacking Platoon was somewhat nonplussed to see a huge Belgian flag suddenly appear out of the upper window. The Piat was also too much for the Germans who ran out at the back and No.15 Platoon entered the house to be met by the very relieved Corporal Thomson and Private Dawson. While occupying this house during the previous day, and while sharing it with the Germans, the snipers had done some valuable work and were awarded the D.C.M. and M.M., respectively.

The bridgehead at Aart was probably one of the fiercest defensive engagements in which the Battalion had yet taken part. The German artillery training school in the Turnhout area, with guns of all types manned by skilful instructors, could concentrate their fire on the

R.S.M. J. WALLS, M.C.

R.S.M. Walls, who comes from Dumfries, enlisted in the K.O.S.B. on the 6th April, 1922, and saw much service with the Regular Battalions.

He became R.S.M. of the 6th K.O.S.B. on the 23rd November, 1942, and served throughout the Campaign in North West Europe, where his gallantry became a by-word in the 15th (Scottish) Division. For his conduct in the Gheel bridgehead he was awarded his Military Cross.

THE GHEEL BRIDGEHEAD   49

tiny bridgehead scarcely six hundred yards deep and three hundred yards wide at the canal. Counter attacks by forces varying from a company to two battalions were constantly being launched from one side or the other. Shelling was persistent, accurate and intense, and in the early morning of the 17th September we reported that we had had 91 casualties in the last twenty-four hours. At 1343 hours the eyes of all were gladdened by the grand sight overhead of the aircraft and gliders which a few minutes later dropped the Airborne Division over Eindhoven, Nijmegen and Arnhem.

During the next morning the Royal Scots Fusiliers were relieved by the 2nd Argyll and Sutherland Highlanders, and the day remained fairly quiet until about 1800 hours when a tank appeared along the track from the west in front of the Carrier Platoon who had been put in position between " D " and " A " Companies. Almost immediately an infantry counter attack developed down the road, supported by more tanks. Observation was poor owing to haze, but the Germans made so much noise as they formed up to attack that we were able to direct our guns and mortars on them. But half an hour later more Mark IV. tanks appeared down the road and a heavy counter attack developed against " A " Company and the carriers, and at the same time a similar attack was launched against the Argylls on the east. While these attacks were forming, the area of the village was subjected to half an hour of the heaviest shelling we had tey experienced. However, by 1925 hours, the Commanding Officer could report, " Fairly hot time, but everything under control," and by eight o'clock the attack had been broken. By now everything was ready for the relief of the Scottish Borderers by the 2nd Gordons, and by four o'clock on the 19th September, the Battalion had recrossed the canal and was on the way back to Gheel.

With the constant counter attacks by day and night while we were in Aart, the consumption of ammunition was enormous, but there was never any shortage of any nature. This was entirely due to the personal efforts of Regimental Sergeant-Major J. Walls who fearlessly crossed and recrossed the canal in an assault boat to feed the Battalion with ammunition under heavy and accurate fire, for the enemy had the crossing exactly ranged with his guns so that no bridge could be built. It was for this bravery and self forgetfulness that the Regimental Sergeant-Major got his well earned Military Cross.

The enemy had shown themselves very sensitive about this bridge-head and had made every effort to eliminate it. But the Battalion held and carried out its orders. In spite of the great number of casualties which we suffered and of the exhausting strain, it is doubtful whether the morale of the men was ever higher. They had done a good piece of work and they knew it. By drawing on itself the weight of the enemy force in northern Belgium, the small British force in the bridgehead had materially assisted the brilliant drive of the 30th Corps towards Nijmegen and the Airborne Division whose landing had so heartened us on the afternoon of the 17th September. The Scottish Division was handsomely thanked by General Horrocks, Commander of 30 Corps, for the help given to his troops by the operation at Aart, and the 6th K.O.S.B. may feel proud of the major part played by the Battalion in the action. Many months later, all who are jealous for the honour of the battalion were proud to learn that the gallantry of the battalion and its commander on this occasion had been recognised by the award to Colonel Richardson of two Belgian decorations in addition to his D.S.O. and Bar won during the campaign.

CHAPTER VII.

THE FIGHTING ROUND BEST.

BARELY forty-eight hours after coming out of action on the Escaut Canal, in which we had lost eight Officers and nearly one hundred and fifty men, the Battalion was again moving up for another engagement. By this time the 7th Armoured Division had taken over the defences of the canal with No. 227 Brigade under command; the 46th Brigade, under command of the 53rd Division, was advancing through Eindhoven and thence north-west towards Boxtel and s'Hertogenbosch. The remainder of the 15th Scottish Division was now ordered to follow the 53rd Division.

On the 21st September the Battalion moved through Moll and Lommel into Holland and harboured for the night in a village called Veldhoven, about five miles south-west of Eindhoven. During the night the Lowland Brigade received orders to place one Battalion at one hour's notice to move as from 0700 hours on the 22nd September, and the other two Battalions at two hours notice, with the probable task of crossing the Wilhelmina Canal at Oirschot and capturing Boxtel and St. Michel Gestel, but the events did not unfold themselves so easily. On the 22nd September, the 46th Brigade made a crossing over the canal astride the road Eindhoven-Boxtel, but found the village of Best strongly held. The 2nd Glasgow Highlanders had particular difficulty with the factory beyond the railway on the west of the village. The 44th Brigade was therefore ordered to move to an area north-west of Eindhoven and to harbour clear of the road, except for the 6th K.O.S.B. who, coming under command of 46 Brigade, were to be ready to follow a squadron of the Reconnaissance Regiment across the bridge.

With the Battalions of that Brigade all engaged in stiff fighting south of Best, however, it was decided to use the Borderers to attack from the east. Crossing the canal in the late afternoon, the Battalion did a wide flanking movement through the woods on the north bank where a few days previously the paratroops had dropped, and starting from the west edge of these woods, attacked just before dark. By 2040 hours the Battalion was in the area of Steenweg, on the east of the main road, except for " D " Company which had gone a considerable distance beyond its objective, to a point about eight hundred yards further north where the woods crossed the main road. Here they remained, unknown for a long time to the enemy, many of whom innocently came down the road on foot, on bicycles or in cars, to be quietly " put in the bag." But the secret was broken when a German patrol jumped into the trench in which Captain Mark Wells was and captured him. On the road to captivity, however, he led them past the trench of Major Coke who promptly captured them all.

Our task for the next day was to clear the road running west from Steenweg as far as the railway by 0900 hours, so as to assist the 46th Brigade who were to capture the southern part of Best. The Reconnaissance Regiment would at the same time begin to push northwards towards Boxtel. The Squadron crossed at about 0700 hours, but were unable to get past a road block defended by infantry and an S.P. gun two miles further north. After an artillery concentration on our objective our attack began. " B " Company was given the task of clearing both sides of the road, with " A " Company on the right. This street was just as doggedly defended as the remainder of Best. All day long the Company wrestled with a most stubborn enemy and gradually Sergeant Kidd's Platoon captured the first four houses, but the fifth was very strongly fortified and by dark only some four hundred yards had been gained in this costly operation.

By now the 8th Royal Scots and the 6th Royal Scots Fusiliers had come up and we reverted to our own Brigade. Early on the 24th September, the 8th Royal Scots began to push northwards along the main road, while the 6th Royal Scots Fusiliers patrolled to De Vleut. But soon the enemy became more active. A severe counter attack came in on the west against the 2nd Glasgow Highlanders, and it was evident that the woods to the north were held in some strength. The 6th Royal Scots Fusiliers were therefore sent to occupy De Vleut, and a plan was made for the 6th K.O.S.B. to advance towards St. Oedenride on the tanks of the 5th Royal Inniskilling Dragoon Guards. While the fighting had been in progress, further airborne landings had been made east of us, and we had been doing our utmost to make secure the main supply route of the 30th Corps through St. Oedenrode and Vechel. At the same time the enemy had been doing all he could to cut off the tip of this salient. In view of the threatened counter attacks, therefore, the operation with the 5th Dragoon Guards was cancelled, and the Lowland Brigade was ordered to take up temporary defensive positions. Later in the day the report was received that the 30th Corps axis had been cut between St. Oedenrode and Vechel by some forty enemy infantry and two tanks.

On the following day the 6th Royal Scots Fusiliers began to move towards St. Oedenrode on foot and by evening met a strong company locality at Donderdonk. It was too late to attack this and the large woods in the neighbourhood, but on the 26th September, 227 Brigade came up on the right, and with the 6th Royal Scots Fusiliers attacked. In the meantime the Reconnaissance Regiment were probing all the tracks in the area and in the afternoon had been to Boschkant and Gasthuishof. The 6th K.O.S.B. was ordered to occupy this area, except for " A " Company which had been sent to protect against sabotage or paratroop landings the bridge over the canal at Zon. It was dark when at 1945 hours the Battalion occupied the area, with " D " Company in the farm north-west of Kremsel, " C " Company at Kremsel with Battalion Headquarters, and " B " Company at Boschkant. Patrols from " B " and " D " Companies found enemy in the farms a few hundred yards in front of their positions, and during the night plans were made for the clearing of these localities on the next day. At 0900 hours " C " Company, under Major Carey, attacked through " B " Company and captured Gasthuishof after an artillery concentration and with the support of a Platoon of Vickers machine guns under Lieutenant Stubbs, the 1st Middlesex Regiment. These latter were then to have helped " D " Company in the attack north-westwards to seize the farm buildings on a slight rise in front of them. They were, however, too late to assist " D " Company who went on without them. This operation began at about 1015 hours, and by 1040 hours the preliminary phase had been completed and the Company was ready to take the buildings. These proved to be strongly held, and as soon as the Company came out into the open, it came under devastating fire of all types and suffered very heavy casualties. The Company Commander, Major Coke, Company Sergeant-Major Melvin and several others were killed, Captain Wells and many more were wounded, and the Company, badly weakened and without leaders, was pinned. Captain Jack Elliot, who was near the Company so as to be able to site his anti-tank guns quickly, immediately took command of the Company, but it was too weak to carry out the assault. When Lieutenant-Colonel Richardson came up to see the situation for himself, he decided that the position was too strong and would need a Battalion attack. Lieutenant Mark Haslam, who had accompanied the Commanding Officer, assumed command of the remainder of the Company, but the urgent task was to collect the many wounded. The Medical Officer, Captain H. R. Thomson, Royal Army Medical Corps, personally directed this work for which a number of Bren carriers had been stripped of all weapons and given Red Cross flags. By a mischance which turned out to be fortunate, he went too far in his carrier and found himself in enemy hands. He was lucky in being able to speak German, for when he had been taken back to the German platoon headquarters, he explained the situation, and after giving his word as an Officer not to speak about what he had seen while in the German lines, he was allowed to proceed with his task. He always said that it was a most eerie experience, knowing that wherever he went he was being covered by a German machine gun not far away. But the enemy honoured his word.

During the day civilians who kept coming to our position reported that the enemy had reinforced Fratershof from Liemde during the night, and as the enemy were stronger than we had at first thought, the attack by the 6th Royal Scots Fusiliers was postponed until dark. But before this could take place, the enemy counter attacked from the north-west, and laid a smoke screen in front of " C " Company. The Battalion was very weak after " D " Company's disaster in the morning. The attack was beaten off, however, and at about eight o'clock " A " Company returned from Zon. At about 2300 hours the Royal Scots Fusiliers attacked, and in spite of heavy casualties, successfully took the position, finding there a reinforced Company well dug in on that dominating feature.

At first light on the 28th September, the 8th Royal Scots attacked Fratershof, which they took after an hour's fighting. The northern flank was now secure, but some doubt existed as to whether enemy held the woods west of us. During the morning, " C " Company sent a patrol to the farm at the corner of these woods and wiped out a position of twelve men. Thereafter, the day was quiet until half past four when a strong counter attack developed between the 8th Royal Scots and ourselves. After a considerable amount of mortaring two companies attacked under smoke, but by 1800 hours the situation was in hand, and something like fifty enemy lay wounded in front of our positions and those of the Royal Scots. A truce was therefore made between the 8th Royal Scots and the enemy and for one hour his stretcher bearers were allowed to collect casualties in the same way as he had allowed the Medical Officer to collect our wounded on the previous day. The next day was fairly quiet, but there was a fear that the enemy would infiltrate between 227 Brigade and ourselves and get to the vital road through St. Oedenrode. So " B " Company was sent to the wood south-west of our main position to prevent this. By now we had heard that soon we would be out of the line and that this time we were to have a long rest. The thought must have been frequently in the minds of many, " I wonder if I shall get hit before we are relieved." And the 30th September was not a quiet day by any means. There was intermittent shelling during the morning, and at 1400 hours a counter attack came from the north-west. This was repulsed with some ease, but again at 1810 hours shelling intensified, especially in " C " Company's area, indicating that more trouble was coming. Sure enough, at 1830 hours a very strong counter attack came against the 8th Royal Scots and ourselves, accompanied by very heavy shelling of the whole area. Again the attack was broken, and by 1940 hours the enemy withdrew. It was his last attack against the Lowlanders. On the following evening we were relieved by the 1st Gordons of the 51st Highland Division, and a depleted and weary Battalion went for a rest to a small village called Boekel, near Gemert, and about eight miles north of Helmond.

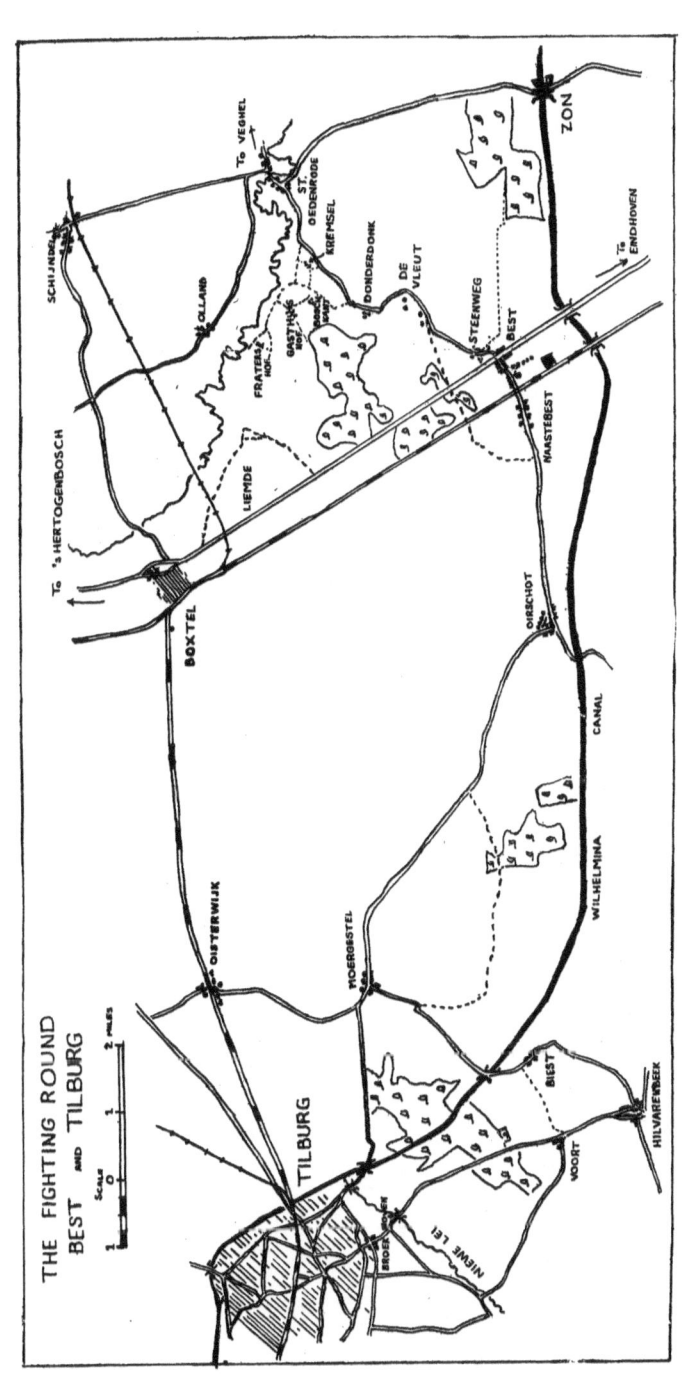

CHAPTER VIII.

TILBURG.

THE Battalion had a rest of three weeks at Boekel, every moment of which was needed to restore the resilience of the tired men who had had but little rest since the first battles, and perhaps more essential, to train new arrivals, to give the new leaders assurance and knowledge of their men and to fashion both into a cohesive, confident fighting force. In that pleasant little Dutch village we had the opportunity to refresh ourselves in comfortable surroundings and peace though the guns could be heard rumbling in the distant Maas, and time to train and perfect our technique of attacking under smoke. We also made all the preparations for a highly secret attack south of Weert from the sector held by the American 7th Armoured Division, which included some most valuable reconnaissances of the canal, which we expected to cross, by Sergeant Holloway and others. On one occasion, while using the American position on the extreme south of their sector as a base from which to patrol, our party was surrounded by a German patrol which had crossed the canal. Our patrol lay quiet and very anxious, for the last orders given to them were that on no account were they to allow the enemy to gain any idea that the 15th (Scottish) Division was interested in the sector. But the raid passed without the enemy stumbling upon this vital identification.

However, the next operation was not to be on that sector. On the 24th October the Battalion moved back to Best, preparatory to advancing on the north bank of the Wilhelmina Canal and eventually attacking Tilburg. The 44th Lowland Brigade was on the left and the 46th Brigade was on the right, moving along westward north of the road through Moergestel to Tilburg. Our task was to clear the canal bank. We did not know what the enemy dispositions were, and did not expect a substantial battle; but we were prepared for small pockets of enemy and endless obstructions in the shape of mines and demolitions. Early on the following morning we began to advance with a troop of the Reconnaissance Regiment leading, followed closely by "D" Company under Major Elliot. Soon, however, it became apparent that the armoured cars could not make any progress along the towpath which, every 50 yards or so, was cut by trenches leading from the scrub on the north side to positions on the water's edge. So by about 0915 hours they returned to the right to use the road along which the 8th Royal Scots were advancing, and "D" Company took the lead. It was difficult enough for the carriers to make progress. Tactical Headquarters could only make progress at all behind a fatigue party consisting of the Commanding Officer, the Second-in-Command and the Intelligence Officer, who ran ahead filling the trenches with brushwood, planks, sand or anything on which they could lay hands. The pace was slow, but, solely due to the ground, as no enemy appeared, and when " D " Company made contact with the Princess Irene Brigade across the canal at Hoogehaghorst at midday, both they and the lock-keeper reported that the enemy had gone. An hour and a half later the road from Biest to Moergestel, which was our objective, was reached. We had had an entirely unopposed advance, but some sharp fighting had taken place on the 46th Brigade front.

The next task was to take Tilburg itself, and this involved moving the Lowland Brigade to a position on the other side of the canal south of the town, from which it could attack while the 46th Brigade attacked from the east. The harbour parties which went to Voort on the afternoon of the 26th October had an eventful journey. Crossing the bridge at Biest, the parties took a reasonable track leading past the demolished windmill straight to the allotted area. That doyen of harbour party leaders, Captain Elder, got past safely, but the second jeep carrying " B " Company party went over what was believed to have been an " R " mine and was blown up. Captain Lountain was badly " concussed " and was lucky to escape with his life, while the driver, Private Young, and Private Renton were both flung some forty yards from the spot and were killed instantly. Private Renton was a great loss to his Company Headquarters. All through the campaign he had been Company Runner, and always, in even the worst conditions, he was to be seen carrying his important messages without a thought for himself. Cheerful, efficient and courageous, he had been all that a Runner should be.

With this incident as a warning, it was decided to send a party of Intelligence Section and Pioneers to sweep the path through the woods along which the battalion would have to pass on the following morning. No mines, however, were found on the axis and all was ready for the attack on the 27th October. The situation in Tilburg itself was unknown. A company of the Princess Irene Brigade was in position north of the wood and they had attempted to enter the town during the afternoon of the 26th October, but had met determined opposition and had suffered several casualties. At about seven o'clock in the morning of the attack, an armoured patrol of the 4th Armoured Brigade had confirmed reports that the enemy were in the outskirts of Broekhoven, a southern suburb of Tilburg, and aerial photographs showed a ring of defences round the town which, if manned, would be formidable. So it was decided that the attack should be preceeded by a barrage and accompanied by a very flexible

Private J. RENTON

Private Renton, who comes from Galashiels, landed with the 6th K.O.S.B. in Normandy as "B" Company Runner. He was killed by a mine on the 26th October, 1944.

Private Renton's invariable cheerfulness, devotion to duty, and intrepid spirit marked him as a man of the highest moral value, and as possessing all the best qualities of a soldier and Borderer.

fire plan. On the right the 6th Royal Scots Fusiliers with their flank on the canal opened the attack at 1100 hours. They were to clear the woods bordering the canal and then the two-battalion assault on the town, with the Fusiliers on the right and the Borderers on the left would be launched with the support of the tanks of the 6th Guards Tank Brigade and " funnies " of the 79th Armoured Division. The 6th Royal Scots Fusiliers met some fierce opposition as they reached the edge of the woods, but dealt with it quickly·

Meanwhile, we had moved through the woods astride the road from Hilvarenbeek to Tilburg, and had formed up for our attack in an orchard held by the Dutch forces. Battalion Headquarters was a short distance behind in a farm which overlooked a wide stretch of open country on the left. While waiting for the main attack to begin, the ever-watchful Lance-Corporal Pleasant spotted some white objects in a hedge about five hundred yards to the left rear of Battalion Headquarters—no doubt a few enemy wanting to surrender. But there was no point in taking risks when one knows that there is often the one man who takes a last shot before surrendering. The section of carriers with Headquarters, therefore, went off to capture these stragglers. They were given clear orders, and made their approach with careful speed, each covering the others, only to find no white flags, but a Platoon of machine-gunners reading the morning papers!

The main assault began a few minutes after 1300 hours, but the ground was crossed by innumerable deep ditches full of autumn rain, through which the assaulting troops, " A " and " B " Companies, had to scramble, so that it took an hour to reach Broekhoven. Tanks could not help as the bridge over the Niewe Lei had been blown. Broekhoven was eventually reached with no opposition, and in spite of the terrifying barrage, civilians flocked round the liberators, and the Commanding Officer's conference beside the road at the entrance to the built-up area was somewhat disturbed by civilian exuberance. At this time sounds of jubilation were heard from the centre of the town, and with the aid of our invaluable interpreter, Sergeant Vogelaar, who had joined us at Boekel, we learned that the Germans had gone and the town was clear. The Colonel, therefore, decided to see for himself, and, incidentally, if the report was really true, to find some good billets. The carrier " Tweed " had a full load of " G ", " A " and " I " representatives to meet all eventualities. The Commanding Officer, Captain Elder, the Intelligence Officer, Sergeant Hunt with his wireless sets, and Corporal Dyson all climbed aboard and, escorted by Lance-Corporal Fairbairn on his motor-cycle, the party set off in the best liberation style. At first it was comparatively easy, but news seemed to spread like sparks in the stubble, that British soldiers were entering the town, and the carrier reached its destination more by the instinct of Private Tracey, the driver, than by the Intelligence

Officer's map-reading. When at last it voluntarily came to a halt at the railway station, it was immediately submerged in a mass of cheering, laughing, weeping citizens, shaking hands, producing scraps of paper for autographs, and being thoroughly continental in their welcome. Battalion Headquarters can claim once, at any rate, to have reached the objective first and to have gone back to guide the remainder of the Battalion.

It was dark by the time the whole Battalion had got to its vulnerable points and billets, and the enemy situation was uncertain, so it was not possible to join the celebrations of the citizens. It was, indeed, necessary to search certain places very carefully, and in spite of a close search, one billet did blow up three weeks after we had left. But on the next day it was considered desirable and justifiable to enjoy a Saturday relaxation, which enabled the citizens to give to the Scottish Division a taste of that welcome which they have extended ever since. Liberation parties were everywhere, in the houses, in the cafes, happy people danced in the streets long after curfew, and hardly a Jock was to be found.

CHAPTER IX.

Restoring the Line of the Maas.

The cup of liberation was rudely snatched from the lips of the liberators before they had had time for more than a sip. While the Division was capturing Tilburg, a successful enemy counter-attack was launched against the American 7th Armoured Division who were holding the line south-east of Helmond, and by now it threatened the second Army Headquarters in that town. The day after Tilburg was taken, 227 Brigade were ordered to the Helmond area as Army reserve, a measure which cast the shadow of future events across the sunny cheerfulness and hospitality of liberated Tilburg. However, it was decided that there is no time like the present, and after the Pipe Band had beaten Retreat in front of the station before a crowd of delighted citizens, it was justifiable to relax somewhat. Only the Adjutant and the Intelligence Officer were immediately available when we received the order, " Move to-night to take up defensive position area Deurne as early as possible to-morrow preparatory to throwing back enemy counter attack. K.O.S.B. cross start point 0200 hours." So at 0200 hours on the 29th October, the 6th K.O.S.B. led the Brigade out of Tilburg, driving all through that bright, frosty night back into the line and a week of hard, continuous fighting.

We arrived at Deurne at about eight o'clock in the morning to find the East Yorks, whose positions we were to take over, champing at the bit to get away and fill a weak place in the line a little farther east. They did, however, stay long enough for the cold and sleepy Borderers to have breakfast before pushing through the tank screen of the 15/19th Hussars to positions on the south side of the thick woods astride the Deurne-Meijel road about three miles south of Deurne.

The situation was very confused. Units of the 3rd Division and the 11th Armoured Division had been put into the line, as available, to prevent any expansion of the German bridgehead west of the Canal de Deurne, and we came under command of the 11th Armoured Division until 15th Division arrived in toto later in the day. The country was close and well wooded, and details of the enemy strength and positions were not known. Every copse was a potential danger. One thing was clear, the enemy was holding Liesel in strength. Five Tiger tanks had been reported there at midday and ten more at Heitrak moving northwards. The American Combat Command B also reported enemy tanks to the east of the main road. The Colonel, therefore, decided the best use of what anti-tank grenades we had, was to lay a minefield on our exposed eastern flank. In order to save time, the grenades were primed and loaded on to a carrier to take them to the place where they were to have been laid, but the heat of the engine caused the grenades to explode and the whole carrier was blown up. To add to the gloom of the day, the Luftwaffe bombed the road in the area of Battalion Headquarters just after dark with high explosive and anti-personnel bombs. One high explosive missed the Regimental Aid Post by a few feet, but blew off the roof, and the Medical Officer, Captain Thompson, caught a small splinter in his nether regions, though he was fortunately not seriously wounded. The Quartermaster too, who was bringing up the rations at the time, had a narrow escape when a bomb landed a short distance in front of his truck.

By six o'clock the situation was clearer. The 8th Royal Scots and the 6th Royal Scots Fusiliers were astride the road Asten-Liesel about a mile west of Liesel, with the 2nd Glasgow Highlanders, now under the command of 44 Brigade, coming up on their right. Further south-west, 227 Brigade were forward of Asten on the road to Meijel, while on the left, the 46th Brigade, with the 6th K.O.S.B. under command, was astride the road Deurne-Liesel on the line of the woods some two thousand yards from Liesel. The Americans had reported that the enemy were withdrawing from Liesel, but a party of the 6th Royal Scots Fusiliers found it still very strongly occupied by active Germans, who had positions among the burning houses. It would be inaccurate to give the impression that the Battalion fought in bad weather conditions, in fact, most of the days were bright and sunny, but in the memory, this period of action remains as a picture of dull atmosphere, approaching night and a countryside lit by innumerable burning farms and stacks leaving in the morning light gaunt charred witnesses of the destruction of war. Confirmation of the enemy's determination to hold Liesel came from a prisoner of the 115 Panzer Grenadier Regiment of 15 Panzer Grenadier Division whom we caught in Loon. He said that his company was in the area of Liesel and that there were some Mark IV tanks among the houses.

During the 30th October the Battalion pushed southwards to occupy Loon, while the 6th Royal Scots Fusiliers attacked Liesel from the west, and the 2nd Glasgow Highlanders engaged the enemy in Slot, a group of houses just south of the village. Our role was to go through Liesel and capture Slot when the Fusiliers had succeeded in their operation. But Liesel proved to be an extremely tough nut to crack. Resistance was particularly fierce round the church, and very heavy shelling and mortaring made progress slow. At 1630 hours the Royal Scots Fusiliers reported that although they had reached the road on the northern outskirts of the village, they were fully committed in mopping up and would not be able to reach their final objectives that day. No sooner were they in position than the inevitable counter attack developed against them from the east. It also hit our forward troops, but apparently by accident rather than by design as the enemy platoon with its supporting tanks quickly turned away. During the night the enemy relieved the Panzer Grenadiers by a battalion of Parachute Regiment Hubner, but the tanks remained. A prisoner caught during the night said that the Germans were building three new bridges over the canal which would be capable of carrying Tigers and Panthers to augment the existing bridges which would only carry Mark IVs. This may well have been a propaganda report as no heavier tanks were met in subsequent operations. More intense shelling accompanied the 7th Seaforths as they passed through us to attack Liesel from the north early in the morning of the 31st October, and it was not long before they reported that the main axis was blocked with destroyed vehicles. Eventually, the village fell about 1300 hours, but there were still considerable numbers of enemy in the neighbourhood, and the 9th Cameronians reported at least three companies in front of them as they moved up on the east of the road to conform with the Seaforths.

The operation to restore the line pushed back by the original counter attack took the Battalion across the enemy's main front behind the canals to the east, from which his gunners had very easy observation of our progress from across the flat fields east of the main axis of advance. And the road along which we moved was well within the range of his guns and mortars. The result was that every step made in the advance was made under well-aimed fire. Liesel itself was a veritable inferno. At about 1500 hours the battalion was ready to attack. The start line was the south end of the village where the main road bent southwards round the windmill from which a whole platoon of Germans emerged to surrender just as we were forming up to attack. " D " Company, commanded by Major Elliot, M.C., was on the right, with " B " Company, under Major Tinniswood on the left., Their task was to take Slot, after which " A " and " C " Companies would pass through, " A " Company to a wood on the right of the road beyond Slot, and " C " Company to a group of farm buildings slightly forward and to the left of " B " Company. After a preliminary bombardment the attack began. It had not to cover a great length of ground, but soon after leaving the start line both Companies came under intense mortar fire, and " D " Company was virtually pinned by fire from tanks in the houses at Slot. Artillery fire failed to move the tanks so Lieutenant Wood stalked one with a Piat and scored a hit with his first shot, and the tank, a Mark IV, burst into flames. On the left the supporting

Churchills of the Coldstream Guards hit another and the advance could be resumed. Very soon after knocking out this tank, Lieutenant Wood was wounded, but he calmly disposed his Platoon correctly before handing it over to his Platoon Sergeant and reported the situation to the supporting tank commander before he allowed himself to be taken back. He was awarded the Military Cross for his gallantry on that day.

So many fires were blazing in the neighbourhood that night that "Monty Moonlight" was practically unnecessary, and both sides remained quiet except for their guns and mortars. A patrol from "A" Company crept out to find whether the enemy was holding the road junction just in front of them, where a small road led eastward to Helenaveen, and found it clear. This augured well for the operations the following day. During the morning the Battalion edged forward down the road to cover the road junction, and, still leading, were ordered just after midday to go on to Heitrak. But soon afterwards the Reconnaissance Squadron with 46 Brigade found strong enemy positions stretching across the axis from Klein Heitrak eastwards to the Hoogebrugge over the Canal de Deurne. By this time the Battalion had suffered several casualties since leaving Deurne, and was tired after continuous fighting which had left us forward Battalion each night. The General, therefore, ordered that we should not be used for further operations that day. But we still remained with our noses in front of the British line, and returned to the Lowland Brigade only to receive the task of capturing Neerkant on the 2nd November. Heitrak was captured during the morning by the 6th Royal Scots Fusiliers and the 2nd Glasgow Highlanders and from the area of "Piglet Farm" just behind their forward defence lines, where the arrival of battalion Headquarters practically coincided with the arrival of an enormous litter of pigs, hence the name, we launched our attack on Neerkant with the 8th Royal Scots on the right. Their task was to clear the woods on the west of the road while we took the village. It was by no means an easy task. The woods on the right were thick pine woods with a single track through them, and the village itself stood slightly higher than the flat, open fields stretching away to the canal and beyond to the east. The main difficulty to be overcome was the same intense gun and mortar fire which had been the feature of the whole squeezing process of the past few days. This fire was particularly intense in the neighbourhood of the church at Neerkant, a fact which at least suggested that there would not be much energetic ground opposition. "A" and "C" Company's made a left flanking movement from Heitrak, which brought "A" Company in the neighbourhood of the church, while "C" Company went farther south to the farms at the edge of the village. At the same time "B" and "D" Companies and Headquarters followed the Royal Scots through the first part of the track through the woods to take the west and south-western part of the village, with " D " Company finishing their advance at Moosdijk. What a journey it was ! The track was not good and, as a minefield had been met in the Heitrak area, it was considered an unnecessary risk to get off the track into the wood, particularly as there were mine boxes here and there. Furthermore, the shells bursting in the trees were worse than those bursting on the ground. And the enemy, appreciating that we should use the track, mortared it consistently. It must have been one of the more exciting moves made by Headquarters as Lance-Corporal Fairbairn, calmly riding his motor cycle, guided them to the hovel selected by the inevitable chalance and Sergeant Hunt's persistence as he demanded reports Captain Elder as a Headquarter. Lance-Corporal Fairbairn's nonof signals amid the heaviest showers of bombs were quite outstanding. For many hours the enemy did not leave that track alone for long, as was brought to the Commanding Officer's notice when he was forced to go to ground and seek the questionable shelter of a " midden " on his way to " D " Company soon after arriving.

Civilians, who had stayed in the village, said that the enemy's tanks had left the previous evening, but that he still held positions a few hundred yards south of the village, as well as in Hof and Meijel further south. An attempt was made by the tanks and armoured cars to get on as quickly as possible and to keep up the impetus of the attack. But a Churchill and an armoured car both hit mines a short distance in front of our positions. A patrol sent out during the night found no enemy within eight hundred yards of our forward defence lines, and established the existence of a minefield across the road. Behind this the enemy appeared to be in well sited positions from which they could sweep the flat open ground with machine gun fire. Any movement forward of our positions brought an immediate and energetic reply from the enemy, and an attempt to recover these vehicles at about eight o'clock on the following morning, under smoke, called forth a tornado of fire of all descriptions. Captain Dudley Shaw, Royal Artillery, who went with the rescue party as Forward Observation Officer, reported shells literally bouncing off his tank.

With the 46th Brigade committed on the Canal de Deurne and preparing to take Helenaveen, and 227 Brigade still on the northwest edge of the wide peat moors which stretched for half a dozen miles west and south-west of Neerkant, it was decided that the Lowland Brigade should take Meijel and clear the country up to the canal. The 6th K.O.S.B. were to carry out a small local operation on the left to form a start line from which the 6th Royal Scots Fusiliers were to attack De Schelm and De Schans. The 8th Royal Scots were then to take Meijel and we were to take "Diamond Wood," northeast of Meijel. At midnight on the 3rd November the 6th K.O.S.B. began the preliminary operation which brought "B" Company level with "C" Company and "A" Company on the extreme left facing south and east. Mines were found in "A" Company's new area, but only one casualty was suffered. There were abundant signs of recent occupation of the area, but no enemy were there when the Company arrived. The 115th Panzer Grenadier Regiment was still in front of us though, and only two or three hundred yards away. In order to allow more adequate counter battery preparations, the attack by the Brigade was postponed until the morning of the 5th November. Meanwhile, the near presence of the Panzer Grenadiers did not make for comfort, and a position about one hundred and fifty yards in front of Sergeant Lee's Platoon was particularly offensive. During the night Corporal Millar took a patrol out from this Platoon to deal with the position. Creeping silently towards the house, Corporal Millar and Private Potts found the sentry in the nearest slit trench asleep, with his Spandau on the top of the trench, Corporal Millar seized the gun and opened fire on the enemy with it, while Private Potts threw a grenade into the trench. It was estimated that four or five Germans were in that trench. Meanwhile, Corporal Stone had taken part of the patrol round the house in time to deal equally effectively with the rear positions and some enemy who came out of the house. Altogether about a dozen Germans were accounted for in the action, but the position was too strong for the patrol to deal with, particularly as the track leading north-east from the farm to the canal was also manned. So, the patrol withdrew, taking the spandau with them.

Early on the 5th November the Brigade attack began. Tanks of the 4th Tank Grenadier Guards in support of the Brigade made a gallant effort to sweep round to the canal in front of us, and then between "Diamond Wood" and the canal, but the ground was too wet and it was not long before fourteen of their tanks were out of action, either by being bogged or through running on to the minefield which stretched across the front. Some very nearly reached "Diamond Wood," an amazing exhibition of their grim determination to help the infantry which had previously made the Lowlanders so fond of them. Deprived of their tanks, the 6th Royal Scots Fusiliers made a valiant attempt to get to their objective under the most devastating fire. By 0910 hours the two forward Companies had each got two Platoons in De Schans, but with the reserve Platoons pinned on the start line, their position was precarious, and in the hail of fire it was not possible to recover the tanks to give them any assistance. "A" Company of the 6th K.O.S.B., in trying to conform with the Fusiliers, ran on to anti-personnel mines and had many casualties when they tried to take a house which was surrounded by a minefield. This mined garden was to cause the death of Corporal Malone and Sergeant Gray, both of the Pioneer Platoon, both of whom gallantly tried to go through the minefield to rescue a wounded man. By 1230 hours, with enemy guns, mortars and machine guns commanding the ground front and rear from across the canal, it was clear that further progress could only be made at the expense of enormous casualties, and the operation was cancelled. The 6th Royal Scots Fusiliers withdrew into reserve, and the 6th K.O.S.B. was left as forward Battalion with the 7th Seaforths coming up on the left on the 6th November.

After this setback, the exhilaration of directing the fire of the 4.2 inch mortars so that a direct hit was scored on a 20 mm. gun can be imagined. But although the Battalion had witnessed a temporary setback, it was only indirectly concerned in it, and the reaction was to settle down to a short period of aggressive patrolling, shelling and sniping which more nearly approximated to the conditions of the Great War as any other part of the campaign. On the other hand, the enemy relapsed into a carelessness which gave our Observation Posts the chance they had hoped for. Whether the enemy thought that we had retired, or whether he immediately relieved his forward troops with fresh units is not certain. Probably he did both. At any rate, he came back into De Schans, and a little east of this, north of "Diamond Wood," men were seen digging or standing about with their hands in their pockets—a very dangerous thing to do under the watchful eyes of Captain Meredith, Royal Artillery, and of the Intelligence Section. A patrol led by Sergeant Hamilton went out during the night, to find the enemy in dug positions in front of De Schans. They all returned safely, but it was a miracle, for they had gone straight through a minefield which was later discovered to consist of one row of Tellermines, one row of "S" mines, three rows of "R" mines, then a gap followed by three rows of Tellers.

When the Battalion came back to this area on the 10th November, after two days rest at Helmond, the enemy were still holding the same positions which he was thought to have strengthened with more mines. The dismal moors were taking on an eerie fascination. One afternoon, just after the misty sun had set and the dark stillness of night was beginning to creep over the desolate fens, a curious light appeared near the most distant of the derelict tanks. It went out, then appeared again and out. Was the enemy using the tank as an Observation Post and some careless observer using a torch to read his map? Or was some observer, weary of gazing over the unmoving scene, having a cigarette before finally leaving his hide? Whatever was the explanation, a light appeared for four seconds in a tank which had lain there, deserted, for the past fortnight. After dark, a patrol went with a Sapper to find out the state of the main road to Meijel. They found mines round the armoured car, and the Churchill and lifted two " T " mines beyond them. They too heard a queer rattling of tins, low whistles as of signals, and saw two round lights in the neighbourhood of the furthest tanks. The enemy was presumably laying mines, but what the lights were was never discovered.

There had been rumours and reports of an enemy withdrawal. Such things we knew of old, but this time the general indications did point to this conclusion, and Lieutenant-Colonel Richardson decided to send a standing patrol into Meijel to remain there during the next day and to return after dark. After a minute study of the air photographs, Lieutenant Maconochie and Private Wood of the Intelligence Section set out at about 2200 hours on the 12th November. They stole out through " D " Company on the right, intending to follow the path taken by previous patrols who had visited a certain point on the moor alternately with the Royal Scots on the west, so as to make a wide sweep round the minefield and into Meijel from the west. At first, they moved easily, but slowly. Then, about midnight, the searchlights, used to give movement light, lit up the whole countryside for miles, at the very moment when the two were crossing one of those tiny rises, imperceptible in daylight, but which at night, under movement light, seem like hills ; and the lights were immediately behind them. There was nothing to do but lie still until the searchlights went out two hours later. On they went again, everything still except for the German guns which every clock hour fired a salvo of 16 to 20 rounds, and a great explosion at 0300 hours nothing but silence and innumerable wire fences. Suddenly, voices and a light from the farm near the farthest tanks. Were the enemy still there then, or was the Observation Post right yesterday in saying that a civilian had been seen walking in that farmyard ? Carefully they crossed the road, over the first line of trenches then over the second and into the back gardens of the block of houses in the main street which they had chosen for an observation post—gardens honeycombed with dug-outs, but deserted. It had been a long, tiring patrol, and it was not until 0610 hours on the 13th November that they crept into the upper storey of the house they had selected. An uncanny silence was over the town. From their observation post they commanded the centre of Meijel and the roads running east and south, but not a movement was seen, nor a sound heard until the deep silence of the house was broken by the clatter of pots and pans, and then the reassuring voices of a woman and children. Still no signs of enemy. Soon after midday a man with a girl on each arm emerged from a house and skipped down the street singing. Gradually the citizens came out, furtively at first, then more confidently, relieved that at last the Germans had gone.

At any rate, a rather hysterical woman who walked into the Royal Scots' lines about this time said they had gone back over the canal during the night. At 2000 hours that night the patrol returned, to confirm with their sober report our hopes which had been reinforced earlier in the day when the fog lifted, and an astonished observation post team reported that Meijel windmill had disappeared during the night.

On the following morning we sent a strong patrol into Meijel, with an 18 set so that they could give a running commentary on their journey.

The log is as follows :—

" 1023 hours. Passing forward troops.
1027 hours. Passing derelict tanks.
1030 hours. Observe enemy lines, unmanned, 70 yards ahead of tanks.
1032 hours. Passing third group of tanks.
1040 hours. Approaching enemy mortar position from the left. Hof now reached.
1053 hours. Civilians in outskirts of Hof report road heavily mined.
1105 hours. Reached railway crossing.
1112 hours. Civilians state enemy left " Diamond Wood " yesterday and went over canal. Not all went. Bridge on road to Beringe blown yesterday.
1125 hours. First cross roads in Meijel reached. Heavily mined.
1138 hours. Area south of church mined and booby trapped. Road west from cross roads mined mostly in puddles.
1205 hours. Reached second cross roads. Heavily mined.
1244 hours. On way back. No enemy, but area extensively mined and booby-trapped."

Patrols were kept in Meijel and Hof while the engineers cleared the axis, and on the 15th November, the forward Platoon, pushing on towards Beringe came under heavy small arms fire from about three hundred yards beyond the second road junction. Apparently the reports of the civilians and of a prisoner that two standing patrols had been left west of the canal were correct. The 10th Highland Light Infantry, who were coming up from the west to take over Meijel, found that some enemy had infiltrated back into the town, and a melee ensued. But eventually the Highland Light Infantry got established and the K.O.S.B. were relieved for forty-eight hours in Asten.

On returning two days later it was found that the 6th Royal Scots Fusiliers had pushed up to the Canal de Deurne in the area of Diamond Wood, and during the day a Royal Scot patrol had confirmed the information given by a prisoner of Battalion Hubner that his company was holding positions on either side of the bridge and between the Canal de Deurne and the Canal de Helena which ran parallel to it about one hundred yards to the east. He also said that the area was so heavily mined that the Germans were not allowed to patrol forward. But big things were also in progress. On the same evening the 51st (Highland) Division opened an attack eastwards south of the Canal du Nord after a big bombardment, and on the morning of the 18th November they were in Beringe. A patrol from " A " Company, consisting of Lieutenant Sweeny and three men, swam across the Canal de Deurne, and found the positions as the prisoner had said, but the enemy had gone. On the 20th November the 9th Cameronians captured Helenaveen and the 49th Division swept through the 51st Division, 227 Brigade pushed on to Vorst and Sevenum, and the Lowland Brigade came into rest.

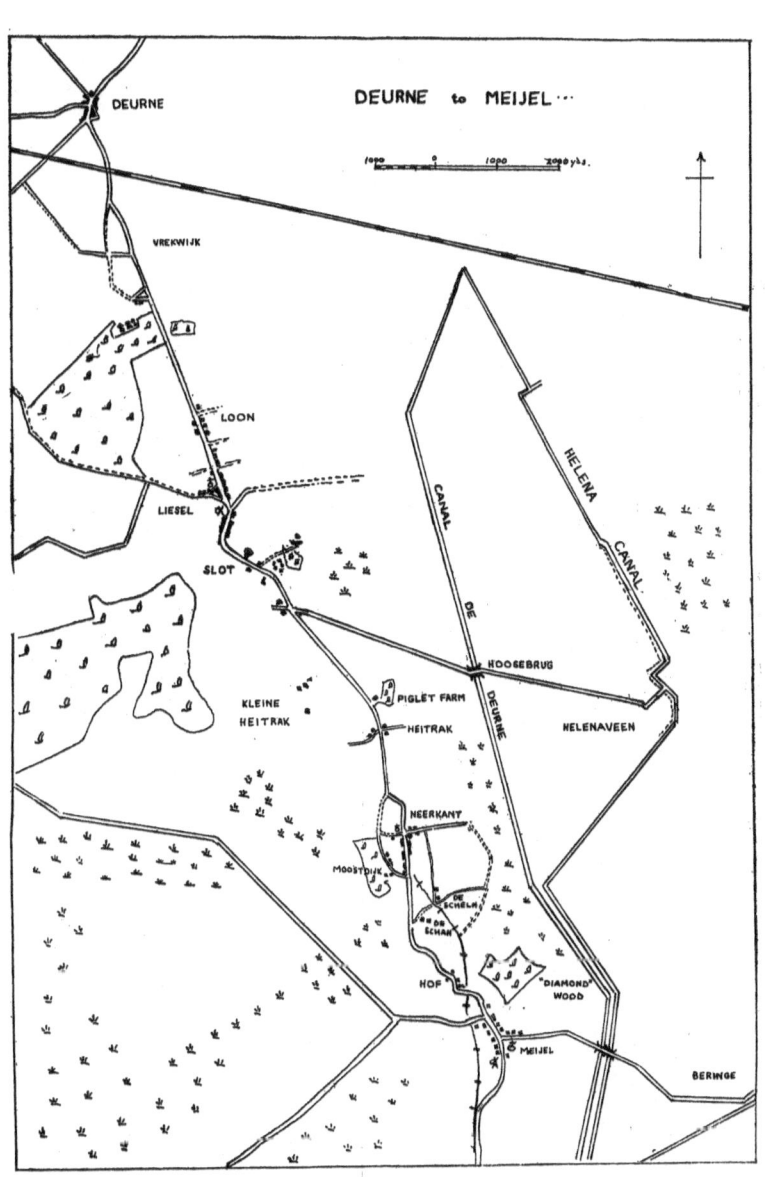

CHAPTER X.

BLERICK AND THE WATCH ON THE MAAS.

THERE was no need for the Battalion to go back for a rest. Almost overnight Neerkant had changed from the front line to a back area, and for the next fortnight we enjoyed a peaceful existence in spite of the ruins. As the village was not on the best road forward, there was comparatively little traffic passing through the area—an occasional American party coming to recover tanks, some gunner trucks and the super-heavy regiment which parked outside our front door on its way forward, giving us the opportunity to admire the huge impressive equipment about which we had heard but which we had never seen. Soon we were to hear them as they helped to prepare for our assault on Blerick.

Blerick, situated in a crook of the River Maas where the railway line from Eindhoven to the Ruhr and to Cologne crossed the river, remained the last German foothold west of the river—a firm base for patrols and a springboard for any counter thrust. The elimination of this last pocket thus became the next task of the Lowland Brigade under its new Commander, Brigadier the Honourable H. C. H. T. Cumming-Bruce, D.S.O., who had assumed command a few days before the attack. The attack, which came to be regarded as a model and the subject of a War Office pamphlet, was a supreme example of how careful planning, organisation and special training can assure success and save lives. It was novel in that it was the first time that infantry, carried in armoured troop carriers, or Kangaroos, had assaulted a town. It was also the Battalion's first introduction to that revolutionary weapon which was to serve us in good stead in subsequent operations. The Brigade Commander insisted on having adequate time for preparation before launching his attack, with the result that, by ample use of cloth models and air photographs, every man knew exactly what was going to happen, and by close training with the 31st Armoured Brigade, every man knew in which Kangaroo he was to travel, and exactly how to stow himself with his weapons and kit.

The Kangaroos undoubtedly saved many casualties during the attack, for the enemy, having retired behind the great river barrier, was guarding it with a large number of guns and mortars, some of large calibre, and it was impossible to assault Blerick without an approach across a considerable space of open country. East of the river, the ground behind Venlo rose sharply and to a height which dominated the almost complete flatness of the country on the west. In addition, Venlo had several buildings from which excellent observation could be obtained over some three thousand yards distance from Blerick. Two churches and the tall Zeiss factory, in particular, gave commanding views. The ground which we had to cross from Maasbree was not quite flat. About three thousand yards west of the town, the tree-covered Blericksche Bergen rose to a height of ninety feet and hid the ground beyond. But once having emerged from those woods on the eastward journey, one felt desperately naked as one moved down the gentle, even slope to the river, one's every movement clear to the eyes which must be watching from the escarpment and buildings beyond.

The perimeter of Blerick was defended by an anti-tank ditch, wire, and, we believed, by mines. Two days before the attack, a Dutch woman managed to get from Blerick to the British line with the information that these defences were manned and that there were between two and three hundred paratroops in the town. This was not unexpected, as we had dealt with their 7th Parachute Division when clearing the other areas, and they were known to be rather tenacious. So the plan was to take the heart out of the defenders before the assault by an artillery programme including the super-heavies and six "mattresses." The guns were then to lift on to Venlo and a counter battery programme. Some were used for smoke. Meanwhile, an armoured force of tanks, flails and Avre bridges were to clear six lanes up to the ditch, lay bridges across it and push on to the outskirts of the town. Two battalions of infantry, the 8th Royal Scots and the 6th Royal Scots Fusiliers, would then drive straight into the centre of the town and burst open the defences. Once this was done, the 6th K.O.S.B. and the 7th Seaforths, who were under command of the Brigade, would attack the southern and northern parts, respectively.

Everything was ready on the 2nd December. One factor alone was uncertain—the weather. The ground on the west of the Maas was soft and the weather had been damp for several days. In the afternoon the rain began. The operation, as planned, depended on the free movement of a great deal of armour over the intervening ground, and the question was, would the ground hold? At nine o'clock in the evening it was still raining, but the Brigadier was determined that the operation should be carried out with or without armour. In the early hours of the 3rd December a reconnaissance party of 31 Armoured Brigade thought that the armour could do their task, and a few minutes after four the Brigadier said over the wireless, "The party will definitely take place." The armoured breaching force did not move off from Rooth until 0800 hours, and shortly afterwards one tank was blown up on a mine, but only scattered mines were found and no definite minefield. It was not until 0930 hours that five of the six bridges had been laid across the ditch owing to the difficult going conditions, but so far shelling was light. As we moved up to our forming-up place at Rooth, and as the 8th Royal Scots and the 6th Royal Scots Fusiliers moved out at ten o'clock, however, the enemy began to shell the area heavily. On the left, the Fusiliers found the ground bad and had to walk most of the way from the ditch, but on the right, the 8th Royal Scots got almost into the town in their Kangaroos, and by midday both Battalions were well inside. Civilians said that the enemy had gone out at eight o'clock that morning, but a prisoner of the 23rd Regiment of the 180th Infantry Division, caught by the Royal Scots, said that his battalion had come into Blerick on the previous day, and that three companies were still there. At 1225 hours " B " Company led the K.O.S.B. attack, with Captain Elder and the Battalion Headquarters' reconnaissance party moving with the reserve Platoon. Major Tinniswood himself seems to have captured the first part of his Company objective round the demolished windmill. Then began the laborious house clearing, while Captain Elder looked for the Headquarters already chosen from the air photographs. Everyone agrees that, in spite of excellent photographs, Blerick was a most confusing town, and before he knew where he was, he found himself on the river bank with only four hundred yards of water and a thin wisp of smoke between his vehicle and the enemy's anti-tank guns. Battalion Headquarters, followed by " D " and " A " Companies came into the town at two o'clock to their respective areas. Mortaring was consistent down that long slope into the town, but no casualties were caused until Major Claud Myburgh jumped out of his Kangaroo which was leading " A " Company and was immediately hit by a mortar splinter. He was the only casualtiy n the assaulting force, though six men of the Mortar Platoon, who were shooting from Hout Blerick, were killed when the cellar in which they were sheltering between shots was hit by two successive 30 cm. " Wurfkorper " bombs which shattered the whole house. Entering the town by an unexpected lane, Battalion Headquarters did exactly what the reconnaissance party had done and found themselves looking across the river at Venlo before discovering where they were. When the little column had been turned with some difficulty, they went back along what was presumed to be the correct street, only to meet a Platoon of Royal Scots clearing it towards the river! It was with some relief that they eventually reached the selected Headquarters. Some time later the Brigade Commander came into Blerick to hold an " O " group, and did exactly the same.

House clearing was a slow process, and as the darkness came on " A " Company, at any rate, continued searching with the aid of matches ! But by eight o'clock the whole area was clear with the exception of the extreme south-west corner of " D " Company's area near the anti-tank ditch where an enemy post was still holding out, to be dealt with by a fighting patrol. By the end of the day fifty-three enemy had been killed, wounded or taken prisoner in our sector alone, so it was more probable that the prisoner's statement was correct and what the civilians said was wrong. These latter, of whom there were three or four thousand in the town, had been living in their cellars for days and only emerged when the town was taken, pale and wretched but smiling. Once the town was cleared, the 8th Royal Scots went back to the Rooth area and the 6th K.O.S.B. was redisposed, with " D " Company on the right round the Concrete Works," B " Company in the centre round the Church, and " A " Company on the left between the church and the bridge. Later, " B " Company took over Hout Blerick from a Company of the Royal Scots which had remained there, and the Carrier Platoon filled the centre of the line. " C " Company at this time was reforming under Major Carey, M.C., in Sevenum.

For a month we stayed in Blerick, first with the 6th Royal Scots Fusiliers, then with the 8th Royal Scots, then again with the Fusiliers until the 22nd December, after which we held the town alone. Although we were entirely static, all that time was very strenuous ; vigilance could never be relaxed, and during the night it had to be particularly alert. The line of the Maas had been cleared and the troops holding it had therefore been thinned. On the other side the paratroops were very active, and during most nights they sent patrols across to the west side of the river. That we did not do likewise did not indicate any loss of vitality on the part of the Scottish Division ; it was part of the big plan for us to remain quiet. It was a period during which all the arts of concealment and observation, handed down from the Great War, could be practised and developed— a period of observation posts and exact shelling and mortaring. Both sides had excellent observation and each shelled the other consistently and accurately. From our observation posts we could watch the enemy going about his daily routine, see him going for his meals, collecting his rations and even observe him zeroing his rifles. His positions south of Venlo could be plotted and estimated with some accuracy, and many of his soldiers were extraordinarily careless in the way they moved about their positions. In the town of Venlo he was rather more sensitive. During the night all sorts of mysterious noises could be hear. The concrete works opposite " D " Company were always a centre of noise and were treated accordingly. Elsewhere, engines could be heard, transport detected on the road beyond the escarpment, probably forces being regrouped for the offensive in the Ardennes, while in the town itself there was endless hammering. It was no unusual thing to see a screen built across a street when daylight broke. Then the game was to knock it down with low trajectory weapons. And all the time there was shelling and counter-shelling, mortaring and retaliation, and incessant "shellreps." They were so numerous that Captain MacDonald inaugurated a "Shellrep League," the results of which were published in the daily intelligence report, with the result that many good bearings were obtained on the enemy mortars. Accuracy brought its own prize. As time went on heavier weapons were used. It is doubtful whether anyone has gone down the cellar steps quicker that Padre Randall did the first time a volley of 30 cm. mortars came over. But it was not altogether his fault—the bottom four steps were missing! On that particular night Battalion Headquarters seemed to be selected as a special target, but it was fortunate that the shooting was rather wild. Several bombs fell in "A" Company's area, and one 276 pound warhead, grazing the corner of a house, struck the road, broke off the tail unit containing the propellant charge and went straight through the window and inside the door of a house opposite, to come to rest, mercifully with a displaced fuse, beside the bed of Lieutenant Spragg who was resting at the time. The tail unit was later found in the bedroom upstairs.

It had been hoped to spend Christmas or Hogmanay in a rest area, so that celebrations could be held with due justice, but this was not possible. Indeed, Christmas Day itself was spent in some tension. For some days previously enemy aircraft had been active over the sector, and civilians crossing from the other side, a constant source of information good and bad, seemed agreed that an attack or at least a large scale raid was planned to celebrate the season, as the Germans seemed to have the opinion that at Christmas time all British troops always got drunk. Rumour had it that 2,000 paratroops had been concentrated behind Venlo, and that the Germans were having their Christmas celebrations before Christmas Day so that they would be able to attack. They certainly did begin early. A day or two before a good deal of merriment, including some girlish laughter, was heard in the direction of the Concrete Works, and during the night of the 23rd-24th December a brass band was distinctly heard by several people. On Christmas Eve church bells were ringing in Velden a few miles north of Venlo, and the strains of "Stille Nacht" and other familiar carols came drifting across from Venlo. The night was indeed still with very little shelling, and civilians who came over the Maas early on Christmas Day reported that the Germans themselves were all drunk and had no intention of attacking. But although civilians brought across very much valuable information, they were not always in a position to know all that was going on in the German lines, and we had no intention of being caught. We could not celebrate Christmas traditionally, so we decided to celebrate, it in our own way. Everyone had a Christmas dinner at midday with beer for those who wished, but after that time alcohol was strictly forbidden. We thought we would have a much better plan than even the enemy; we would persuade him to attack us and then we would destroy him. So, after dark, while two-thirds of the Battalion " stood to " in their positions, and all observation posts were manned, the remainder would organise a bogus jollification after a cup of hot sweet tea, to suggest to the enemy that we really were drunk. Regimental Sergeant-Major Walls, M.C., was to arrange for two large fires to be lit at the back of Blerick, as if the Borderers, in their cups, had got so out of hand as to set even houses alight. Battalion Headquarters' contribution to the general pandemonium was an amateur band, consisting of the Regimental Sergeant-Major, Company Quartermaster-Sergeant Kinnaird, Sergeant Herbert and Private Dewar who had found a drum, a mouth organ, a pair of cymbals and an unknown brass instrument. Pandemonium was in five phases, each Company starting in turn like the singers in a round. The fires were lit and the warriors in the trenches blinked into the darkness to spot the first enemy to come in range. But the Bosche never stirred. Not a shell answered our invitation. Even the fires fizzled and smouldered like damp crackers to burst into flame and pour forth dense clouds of smoke in the broad daylight of Boxing Day just when they were not wanted. We had been sold a pup. We had even gone to buy it ! Perhaps the Germans were still drunk, or perhaps they could not appreciate the deep subtlety of our plan.

Hogmanay, our last night in Blerick, was celebrated in a similarly friendly but more effective way. Captain Moffat, Support Company Commander, and Captain Burnett, the Mortar Officer, devised a " hate programme " to which the gunners were only too pleased to add their contribution. At midnight, every known enemy position and several suspected ones were engaged. This did at least bring an answer in the form of rifle grenades fired across the river, and bursting harmlessly to scatter leaflets, on which was printed, in very very bad English, a message hoping that we had enjoyed the Christmas which we had expected to celebrate at home, and warning us that soon the water of the Maas would be red with the blood of our comrades which would flow down the river and wash the very shores of England. It was quite extraordinary where all this blood was going to flow !

One night shortly before we were relieved, a patrol came over in the remote part of " D " Company's area, but nothing happened and no alarm ensued. However, in the morning, Major Elliot had to report, a trifle diffidently, that a swastika flag had somehow appeared on an unoccupied house on the river's edge in Sergeant O'Neal's Platoon area—a house which could not be reached by day as all approaches were under enemy fire. So the flag had to fly. This was too much for the Regimental Sergeant-Major and Sergeant Stoddart, so as soon as it began to get dark they went to the house, took down the flag and substituted an effigy of Hitler in its stead. Honour was satisfied, but it was a long time before Major Elliot and Sergeant O'Neal lived down the tale of " Castle O'Neal."

After a short rest at Sevenum, where justice was done to the season, we returned to the Maas to relieve the Royal Scots Fusiliers in the sector between Blerick and Grubbenvorst which was held by the 1st K.O.S.B. Representatives from each Platoon spent a day and a night in the new positions before the main body arrived, and it was while on this advance party that Sergeant Ahearn was killed by a mortar bomb. Here the situation was very different from Blerick, where good, comfortable billets could easily be found in the houses. In the new area houses were few, and neither " B " Company on the left, nor " A " Company in the wood next to them, had a single house in their areas. The weather had become very cold and the whole countryside was covered with thick frozen snow. The days were sunny, but the nights were a trial, particularly to the men in the listening posts near the river's edge. Each Platoon had one which was manned by two or three men, frequently relieved during the night. On the whole, the sector was quieter than at Blerick and, with the exception of " A " Company's wood which was frequently shelled, was but little disturbed. The same alertness had to be maintained, and on several nights trip flares in the woods between Battalion Headquarters and the Companies suggested that enemy patrols were about, but it was later found that these flares had been fired by the frost. Patrols certainly did come across, and on the night of the 19th-20th January, the last night before we were relieved, an attempt was made to eliminate a listening post manned by No. 13 Platoon. A small party came over on the right of the post and made enough noise to attract attention. Meanwhile, a larger party of some fifteen or twenty men came over on the left and approached the post from the rear. Fortunately, Private Avery, who was manning the Bren gun, and Privates Buoy and Brown, the others in the post, were very alert and opened fire on the larger party before it could do damage, and having fired all their magazines, withdrew according to orders. Sergeant Thompson then took a patrol to the post, but the enemy had gone. When a sweep of the area was made in the morning one dead German was found and one under a haystack, a tough little creature who had lost half of one foot in Russia, dressed in only a shirt and a pair of trousers. According to him, the boat in which he had come across had sunk on the return journey and the rest of the occupants had been drowned, but he swam back and intended to swim over to the enemy side when it got dark. He was the only prisoner who had been caught for a month, and was hurried back to Divisional Headquarters for immediate interrogation.

On the evening of the 20th January, 1945, we were relieved to go back to Belgium for a real rest, and so ended the last defensive phase of our campaign. It had been a phase of unremitting watchfulness and strain, but by no means as uncomfortable as had been anticipated. All variety of people not normally seen with forward troops visited the area and took the opportunity of looking at the enemy positions perfunctorily. That does not apply to the two Corps Commanders who came. Lieutenant-General Ritchie examined Venlo carefully from our lines in Blerick, and Lieutenant-General Barker carried out an even more detailed examination in the northern sector. Having to leave his car some five hundred yards behind the forward Companies, he elected to cover that distance at the double, an outburst of energy somewhat embarrassing to the Commanding Officer and others who had been leading the semi-troglodyte life of the past six weeks. And this was followed by a veritable fusilade of most searching questions directed at all whom the General met, from the Commanding Officer downwards. Lieutenant Beardmore batted particularly well that day. There were always diversions. One never knew when an unpleasantness of one kind or another would arrive, and even Captain Smith, the Quartermaster, was in the habit of wearing his steel helmet while bringing the rations down that long slope into Blerick every evening. But seven weeks of static life after the rush and excitement of the past months was always liable to produce the reflection which appeared in a higher formation Intelligence Summary one day:

> "As I sit on the banks of the Maas,
> I reflect it is really a farce,
> At my time of life,
> And miles from my wife,
> To be stuck in the mud on my ———"

CHAPTER XI.

THE SIEGFRIED LINE.

GRAMONT was excellent when we arrived there on the 21st January after a long cold journey. Everyone was pleased to get to the gaiety of Belgium after the dreary, depopulated fields of the Maas area, and being only sixteen miles from Brussels was an additional attraction. The next operation in which we were destined to take part, however, was under the command of the 1st Canadian Army, which gave the General reason to move the Division to the area of his beloved Tilburg. Weather conditions prevented an immediate move, but after two or three carefree days in Gramont, we went to Tilburg where the whole Battalion was billeted in a housing estate built since the outbreak of the war, and very soon we were to advance into Germany, to what looked like being one of the biggest operations in which we had yet been engaged: the breaching of the Siegfried Line. Thousands of excellent air photographs and maps, some of the scale of 1 :12500 which had been specially made for the operation, poured into the Battalion, and, as the planning was at the "Top Secret" stage, and known only to the Colonel, the Second-in-Command, Major A. E. S. Jackson, M.C., who had joined us at Neerkant, and the Intelligence Officer, the latter decided to keep them in his bedroom, where long hours of careful planning, drawing and study were spent behind locked doors. A little later, Sergeant Stoddart was admitted to the secret so that his first class draughtsmanship could be utilised. It was often wondered whether the humble civilians who lived there ever realised quite what momentous plans were being devised in that little back room of their house.

Whatever apprehension may have been felt about the magnitude and possible difficulty of the task, quickly gave way to optimistic confidence when Lieutenant-General Horrocks, Commander of the 30th Corps, gave a buoyantly enthusiastic exposition of his plan for operation "Veritable" to all Officers on Sunday, 4th February. 30 Corps, under the command of the 1st Canadian Army, seemed to consist of the major part of the 2nd British Army. The General's *dramatis personae*, showing all the formations, A.G.R.A.s, A.G.R.E.s taking part in the operation, was indeed an imposing list. It was the first time the 15th (Scottish) Division had fought under General Horrocks, and he used the Division as his "centre forward." It was to be an attack on a five-Divisional front. The 51st (Highland) Division was to attack south of the Reichwald, the 53rd (Welsh)

Division had the task of clearing the forest itself, the Scottish Division had to break through the defences of the Siegfried Line between the forest and the road from Nijmegen to Cleve, while the two Canadian Divisions, in Buffaloes, had to clear the marshy area up to the Rhine. Once the Siegfried defences had been pierced and Cleve captured, the armoured Divisions and the 43rd Division were to make a swift drive to seize intact, if possible, the bridge over the Rhine at Wesel, sixteen miles south of Cleve. It remained to be seen what opportunities the enemy would give us, but the General said, " I like an untidy battle," and it was clear that no opportunity would be lost. It was, however, absolutely essential that the roads be kept clear so that, at the right moment, the armour could be launched without any hindrance. Strict orders were given to push into the ditch, any gun or vehicle, even a General's, which broke down. Major-General Barber, Commander of the 15th Division, had the misfortune to have a jeep which broke down, and orders were obeyed.

In our sector the Siegfried defences were not made as formidable with concrete as might have been expected, but consisted of dug positions in depth running back from about the frontier to the anti-tank ditch a thousand yards east of the village of Frasselt. The ditch itself was apparently unfinished, and was neither very wide nor very deep. It was, however, a sufficient obstacle. As far as forces were concerned, it was known that the enemy was short of troops, and it was thought that perhaps he would be prepared to give up the Siegfried Line and hold the great river barrier behind. At any rate, his troops were not good fighting stuff, and would be even less inclined for battle after a barrage of some thirteen hundred guns. They were expected to be holding the forward dug positions and, as our pressure increased, to fall back behind the ditch in front of their billeting area at Schottheide. Quite what the high ground between there and Cleve contained was not known, but the features of Wolfsberg and Hingstberg, about a mile beyond Schottheide, were known to have some positions on them.

The attack was to be launched from Nijmegen at first light on the 8th February. On the 15th Division sector, 46 Brigade and 227 Brigade were to capture the line Frasselt-Kranenburg, after which, 44 Brigade was to re-enact its attack on Blerick against Schottheide and push through to Wolfsberg, Hingstberg and Nutterden. Then one or both of the other Brigades would seize Cleve. The more detailed plan of the Lowland Brigade was for the 6th K.O.S.B., with an armoured breaching force consisting of No. 2 Squadron of the 4th Grenadier Guards, together with flails, crocodiles and Avre bridges of the 79th Armoured Division to start from Frasselt and seize Schottheide. The 8th Royal Scots on the left would then come up and seize the north part of the village and Tuthees. The

6th Royal Scots Fusiliers and the 2nd Gordons, who were under command of the Brigade, were then to go on to the high ground and Nutterden, respectively. For us it was an attack which we quite liked—one which did not involve a very early reveille and a hurried breakfast eaten in the dark. We could hope for a good night's sleep before it, too. But our sleep in Nijmegen was not allowed to be peaceful. At about four o'clock in the morning a big air raid was made on Cleve, Goch and Emmerich, and at six o'clock the barrage opened.

According to the plan, prospects were excellent. One thing alone was incalculable—the weather. Lightning thrusts depended to a great extent on good going conditions, and, once again, rain made the ground most unfavourable, much more so than at Blerick. The marshy nature of the ground was made even worse by dykes being broken by shelling, so that some of the tracks were already quagmires. Stiff fighting took place during the day but steady progress was made to the first objective, and during the afternoon the Colonel was able to go to the Headquarters of Lieutenant-Colonel Remington-Hobbs, now commanding the 9th Cameronians, at Auf dem Hovel on the hill overlooking Frasselt and there make final arrangements for our attack. Colonel Remington-Hobbs guaranteed to clear Frasselt so that we could use the road as a start line, and to give shelter to "C" Company, which was to escort the armoured breaching force while they waited for zero hour. Tactical Headquarters had been forward all day, but the remainder of the Battalion had remained in Nijmegen, waiting to be called forward in Kangaroos. Owing to the condition of the ground and the resultant slowness of progress, they were not called up until about 2100 hours, which was the originally projected zero hour. The first part of the journey was easy, but once Groesbeek was passed the Kangaroos had to go over rapidly deteriorating tracks which had already carried a good deal of armour, and a series of misfortunes to the Avre bridges made progress even slower. They had difficulty in negotiating the trees which lined the roads, and one by one the supports of the bridges snapped so that at one time it looked as though no bridges would ever get as far as the ditch. Having the great bridges lowered in front of the tanks made it even more difficult to move in the ever-deepening mud and round the bends in the tracks, and it was not until 0500 hours on the 9th February that the armoured breaching force could start preparing the lanes. Two flails got bogged almost immediately, and half an hour later three of the proposed lanes were useless. Lane 2, running east from Frasselt church, however, was good as far as the ditch, and a new track was found running south-east from the north end of the road from Frasselt to Schottheide. A few minutes after six o'clock the bridge on lane 2 was working, and soon after "C" Company was ordered across the ditch. The other Companies, unable to move across country to Frasselt, soon followed, using the road through Kranenburg which was held by the 2nd Argyll and Sutherland Highlanders. "D" Company went straight over lane 2, swung right in Schotteheide and sent a Platoon on to the Hevberg feature which dominated the southern part of the village. "A" Company, under Major Malone, took the northern part of the village, and "B" Company, under Major Tinniswood, pushed some distance beyond them and seized some out-lying farms. A prisoner of the Fusilier Battalion of the 84th Division, captured by 46 Brigade, had said that his battalion had one company up in Frasselt with three behind, while the supporting artillery was in the area of Cleve. This proved fairly accurate, but the enemy had no fight left, and Schottheide was occupied with little difficulty. The 6th K.O.S.B. were therefore ordered to push straight on to the Wolfsberg feature without waiting for the Fusiliers who were making slow progress owing to the mud.

"A" Company went straight for this as soon as possible, followed by "B" Company who took a rather wider sweep round the hill. Unfortunately, No. 7 Platoon missed the track and went too far before swinging on to the hill. The leading Kangaroo was hit by a bazooka which killed the driver and wounded the Platoon Commander, Lieutenant Beardmore, and several others. Sergeant Lee, however, quickly reorganised the Platoon, overcame the enemy who had attacked them from the house nearby, and went on to capture the objective with great energy and skill, thereby winning the Military Medal. No. 8 Platoon, meanwhile, captured a troop of four 88 mm. guns, and "B" Company, in an equally successful attack, seized a large dug-out which, judging from the wireless and telephone equipment inside, was a headquarters. They also captured eight officers, including the commander of an infantry battalion and the commander of No. 184 Artillery Regiment. In their clearing operations on the edge of the forest, "D" Company had also taken twelve prisoners of the 1307th Artillery Regiment who were manning a light gun position between the village and the forest. By 1115 hours the total number of prisoners taken had risen to ten officers and two hundred and thirty other ranks.

At this stage, the 8th Royal Scots began to move up to the Hingstberg feature, and the 6th K.O.S.B. were ordered to push right forward, round the tip of the Reichwald, and seize Bresserberg, a feature commanding the approaches to Cleve itself. Here the track ran between two woods, and on either side the widening fields were found to be mined. "D" Company led, picking up "A" and "B" Companies and the tanks on the way, and all speed was made to this vital hill. We arrived only just in time. As it was, there were some sharp engagements on the hill, but had we delayed,

The Siegfried Line

the enemy would certainly have had time to occupy it in strength. More prisoners were taken, but this time from the 7th Parachute Division, and by the time our night positions had been organised we had taken 12 officers and 254 other ranks. The parachutists proved to be very aggressive, and our occupation of the position was disturbed by a strong patrol which worked along the trenches near Battalion Headquarters and attacked the Platoon of medium machine gunners as they were arriving. The position was, however, secured and the enemy forestalled in his attempt to occupy the feature, which was the key to Cleve.

During the early morning of the 10th February, 43 Division began to move along the road through Nutterden with a view to continuing the attack southwards towards Goch. 44 Brigade was therefore ordered to occupy Cleve, starting about midday. It was found, however, that the Watch Tower area was still very much occupied, but the 6th Royal Scots Fusiliers, who sent a party to clear it, reported only six German dead and no opposition there. By this time it was 1800 hours and too late to occupy Cleve. Furthermore, a somewhat confused situation was found in the town, and shortly before eight o'clock the Brigadier reported to Division that one Brigade of the 43rd Division was spread all over the southern part of the Lowland Brigade's objective, that we had been shelled by 43 Division, and that he was arranging to relieve this Brigade at first light, after which we would continue with our task. The battle was indeed getting untidy. Soon afterwards the 6th Royal Scots Fusiliers reported forty enemy dead and twelve taken prisoner during clearing operations in the Watch Tower area.

In the late afternoon enemy armour was seen moving near the cemetery on the south side of Bresserber, and the S.P. anti-tank guns were called forward to deal with it. We were very gratified to have speedy report that one of the enemy vehicles had been hit and knocked out, and everyone carried on with his business. Then an awful rumour arose. The positions of our own flanking formations were a little uncertain, and it was known that the Guards Armoured Division would be operating through one of the divisions on the right. Now the Coldstream Guards had a Panther. Perchance we had knocked out this apple of their eyes, which had survived so many hazards and recriminations since it was captured in Normandy. What would be Major Pike's reputation, or that of any other Grenadier with us, if they had been a party to any such dastardly act!

At about seven o'clock on the morning of the 11th February, reconnaissance parties, under the command of Major Malone, set out on foot for Cleve, but almost at once ran into trouble from the Watch Tower area. Captain Thomas and Lieutenant Welburn were wounded, the former having to be evacuated; Lieutenant Welburn, however, was not seriously wounded, and after pulling a shell splinter from his face, refused to go back as it would leave his Company Commander with no other Officer in the Company. The Fusiliers were again detailed to clear the area with the aid of tanks. These latter proved too much for the enemy, and when the Churchills opened fire over one hundred parachutists surrendered. With the way now clear, the 8th Royal Scots and the 6th K.O.S.B. entered the ruins of Cleve, while the 6th Royal Scots Fusiliers remained on the feature to prevent any further infiltration. Cleve was, indeed, a ruin. The bombing raid, together with the heavy shelling, had cratered every road and considerably damaged every house, so that it was very difficult to find a dry place in which to harbour the troops when they were off duty. And now the enemy began to shell it heavily and accurately. We remained there until the following evening, when we were relieved by the 7th Canadian Brigade after the 129th Brigade of 43 Division had passed through to continue the attack southwards, while the Canadians on their left cleared up to the river. From Cleve we went back to the Bresserberg feature to rest—in a 5.5 gun area ! We had, however, to maintain a certain degree of alertness, as the five hundred infantry with tanks reported at Hau threatened a sizeable counter attack, and two new enemy divisions had appeared, the 15th Panzer Grenadier Division on the left and the 116th Panzer Division south of them.

The general situation was that 53 Division had cleared the Reichwald, and were now holding the eastern edge, but were very tired through sheer physical exhaustion. The 51st Division, with the 52nd Division behind them and on their right, were pushing eastwards south of the forest against the 6th and 7th Parachute Divisions. 43 Division were advancing southwards from Cleve towards the Forst Cleve, and the Canadians were clearing the country bordering on the Rhine. Between them and 43 Division, the 46th Brigade were "to operate vigorously on the axis Moyland-Calcar." The Lowland Brigade were, in theory, in support of the fatigued Welsh Division, in case of possible counter attack, but the order of the day was maximum rest.

There was no question about which side had superiority, but it was unfortunate that conditions were such as to frustrate the speedy advance hoped for in the plan of Operation "Veritable." One thing is certain, that but for the determined advance of the 6th K.O.S.B. to the Bresserberg feature, which forestalled the enemy's occupation of that key position, the advance would have been very much slower and very much more costly. The success was the result of quick appreciation, determination to exploit opportunity and good organisation, and when General Horrocks met the Commanding Officer on the following day, he expressed his satisfaction at the contribution which the Battalion had made to the materialisation of his plan.

The Siegfried Line

Before leaving this part of the story a word must be said about the formidable difficulties which had to be overcome in our rear by the " Q " Branch. Very soon after we had got established across the Siegfried Line, the road through Kranenburg, the only road over which supplies could come forward, became flooded to a depth of several feet, so that supplies had to be sent up by " Dukws." When it is remembered that this was the administrative route, not only for the 15th Division but also for the Guards Tank Brigade and the 49th A.P.C. Regiment working with the Division, as well as the 43rd Division and its attached armour, some idea can be obtained of the vast quantities of food, ammunition, petrol, etc., which had to be brought over it. Yet all through the operation and the next one, the Battalion was never short of a single requirement, a great tribute to the ingenuity and ability of the Quartermaster, who seems to have established a small F.M.C. of his own across the flood.

CHAPTER XII.

GOCH AND SCHLOSS KALBECK.

DURING the next few days the battle moved on fanwise towards Goch, Udem and Calcar. Some difficulty was met in clearing the Forst Cleve, and eventually it was left as a pocket, while the 43rd Division, with the Highland Brigades of the 15th Division on the left, pushed southwards. On the early morning of the 18th February, the 1st Worcesters had halted on the tree-lined escarpment north-east of Goch and were patrolling forward. From here, 44 Brigade had been ordered to attack and capture the town of Goch.

Goch itself stood at the base of a " U," formed by the River Niers, which cut it in half. Three roads ran into the northern half of the town ; the main roads from Cleve and Calcar ran almost parallel to the river, and between them a minor road ran through the clusters of farms south-east of the Forst Cleve. This road and the main road from Cleve were in British hands. Entrance to the town was canalised down them by an anti-tank ditch running along the escarpment, which, however, did not actually cut the roads. On the immediate outskirts of Goch there was a second ditch, some twenty feet deep, which cut both.

The Lowland Brigade, now well experienced in assaulting such positions was ordered to seize this nodal point, and the original plan was for the 8th Royal Scots to attack down the Cleve road, and the 6th K.O.S.B., now under command of Major A. E. S. Jackson, M.C., during the absence on leave of Lieutenant-Colonel Richardson, was to carry out a simultaneous attack down the centre road. Both Battalions were in Kangaroos, and were to be preceded by an armoured breaching force. The 6th Royal Scots Fusiliers were to go through the assaulting Battalions once they had got a foothold in the outer part of the town. It was anticipated that there would be some stiff fighting, and patrols of the 1st Worcesters reported early in the morning a good deal of mortaring and machine gun fire. The Brigadier, however, motored almost as far as the second ditch, wearing his inevitable soft hat and came back quite unharmed, which suggested that resistance might not be as bad as expected. Further patrols of the 43rd Division confirmed this, so the plan was changed, and when the forward battalions arrived in the forward assembly area, near the Forst Cleve, they were ordered to attack as soon as possible and to go through the town as far as the river.

We followed the Royal Scots out of the assembly area at about 1500 hours. The first part of the journey was along the Cleve road, and it was some time before we could branch off along one of the small muddy tracks to get onto our proper axis. The armoured

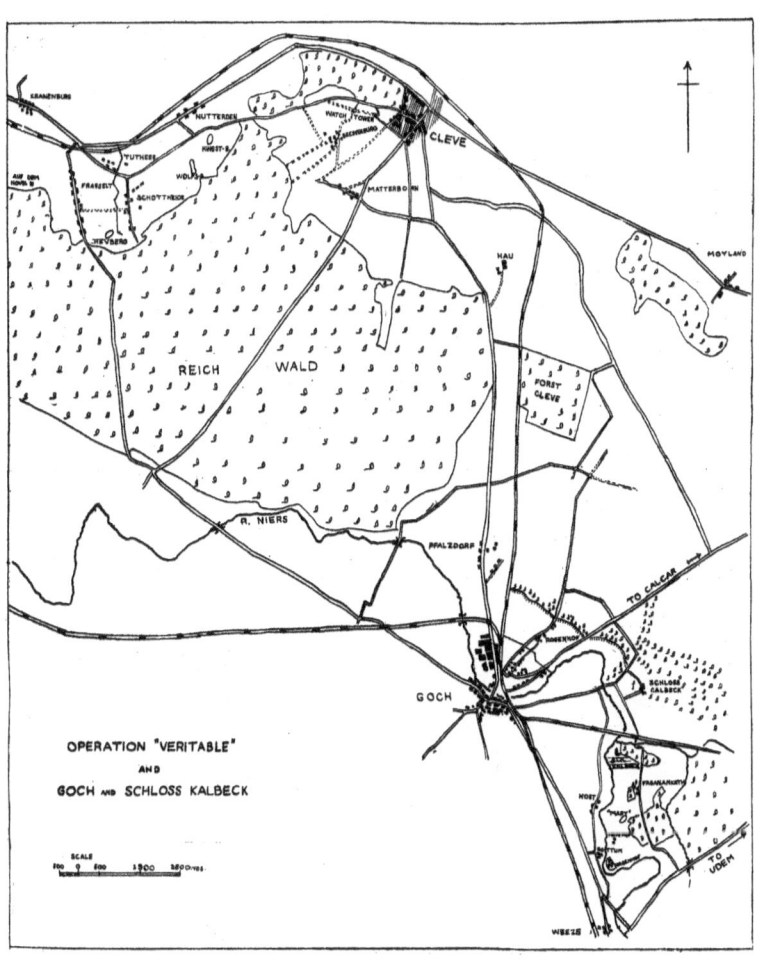

breaching force went ahead and experienced exactly the same difficulties as they had had on operation " Veritable." Conditions were indeed worse because the nature of the ground denied any freedom of manoeuvre, and rain had been falling during the last two days. There was every prospect of a very difficult situation. At 1640 hours the Grenadiers reported that both the bridges on the two Axes had failed to work, though they hoped to rectify this in a short time. But ten minutes later it was apparent that the bridge on our axis would not be effective as the ground was very sandy and the sides of the ditch crumbled. Fascines were immediately called forward. Being out of wireless touch with " D " Company who were leading, Major Jackson went forward in his Kangaroo to see what was happening ; and a very unpleasant journey it was. " D " Company had found shelter in the ditches and houses a short distance from the obstacle ; shelter was very necessary as the enemy were shelling the area very heavily and the shells were bursting in the trees which lined the road. A new plan was then made with Major Elliot and Captain Meredith, Royal Artillery. " D " Company was to get across the ditch on foot after dark, and the other Companies were to follow, with " B " Company working round to the left. As soon as Major Jackson had gone away, Major Elliot and Captain Meredith went forward to make a reconnaissance. No sooner had they got on to the road than Major Elliot was hit by a burst of machine gun fire and was killed. Captain MacNab immediately assumed command of the Company, but the plan was not put into operation. By half-past seven " B " Company was held up on the north edge of the obstacle by machine gun fire from the left, and " D " Company was unable to do more than form a firm base on the near side. Major Jackson, therefore, decided that the only thing to do was to make an entirely fresh plan with adequate preparation and support. Zero hour would be at 2300 hours, when " D " and " B " Companies would assault through the firm base made by " A " and " C " Companies about one hundred yards north of the ditch. By that time it was expected that the bridge would be in operation, so that " D " Company would rush the town in Kangaroos while " B " Company again worked round the left on foot.

    The bridge was laid as hoped, and at zero hour No. 17 Platoon charged into the northern end of the town, followed by the remainder of the Company. On reaching the first group of houses they were attacked with panzerfausts. Three Kangaroos were hit, and Lieutenant Compton, the Platoon Commander, was wounded in the head as he " depouched." The houses were immediately seized and cleared, and the Company remained disposed in a tight position ready to continue clearing at first light. We had got a foothold, and much credit for the success of this spectacular action must be given to the brilliant driving of the Kangaroo drivers who handled their vehicles with such skill on that narrow bridge in the fog and darkness, and to the sappers whose work on the bridge made the operation possible. The bridge itself collapsed, and they had to do a great deal of work on the site before the Kangaroos could get back at 0100 hours on the 19th February. All this time a German 75 mm. gun, sited near to the level crossing in the centre of the town, was firing straight down the road.

Meanwhile, " B " Company on the left was having a long strenuous fight to get their objectives. Starting from the southern part of Rosenhof, they had not gone a hundred yards before they struck a trench system which ran south-eastwards to their objective, on the road Calcar-Goch, at a point where the anti-tank ditch crossed it. This was taken as the axis along which No. 10 Platoon was to move under the command of Sergeant Telfer, with No. 12 Platoon, under Lieutenant Allard, going across the fields on the left. The trench was manned for its entire length by paratroops. No. 12 Platoon was engaged from this trench with rifle grenades, and Sergeant Smith was wounded, but they were not materially affected by these defences. On the other hand, Major Tinniswood, Sergeant Telfer and No. 10 Platoon had to fight a keen bayonet and grenade battle along every yard of the trench. Sergeant Telfer, crawling along the top of the trench, lobbed grenades into every leg of the trench, while the others, advancing inside it, dealt with such enemy as needed attention. It was not until 0225 hours that the objective was reached, and sixteen prisoners of Flieger Ausbild Battalion 45 had been taken. Here they found that the bridge was intact, but that the enemy held the houses across the ditch. No. 10 Platoon seized the first house, but the enemy counter attack prevented them from taking the next one. No. 12 Platoon, who had had to cross the ditch, which was twenty-five feet across and ten feet deep, by jumping inside and then hauling each other out with shovel handles, were now on the left, and No. 11 Platoon were used to attack the second house. They were still not able to dislodge the enemy, and it was decided to use tanks against it in the morning. So " B " Company remained for the rest of the night in and around the first house, with the next house, not 30 yards away, held by obstinate enemy. To add to the tension, the Company was out of touch with Battalion Headquarters. However, Private Beaumont got back to report the situation. The arrival at first light of Lieutenant Gray's troop of Churchills decided the enemy. After the first two rounds, twenty-five scared Germans came out to surrender, one of fine physique, being literally caught with his trousers down to be greeted with roars of laughter from " B " Company. For their gallant conduct in this tough action, Major Tinniswood was awarded the Military Cross, and Sergeant Telfer the Distinguished Conduct Medal.

While " B " Company was fighting on the left, " A " Company, under Major Malone, was passed through " D " Company to the centre of Goch, which they cleared at first light. About midday " C " Company, under Captain Haslam, coming up with support of tanks, cleared the remaining section of the town between " A " and " B " Companies and finished the task. On the 21st February the Highland Division moved across our front south of the river, thus putting us out of the battle for the time being.

The operation had been a commanders' battle *par excellence*. From the very start circumstances had made impossible the execution of cut and dried plans previously studied and mastered, so that the influence of Major Jackson was felt throughout the battle, and to his judgment and skill, above all, must be attributed the success. He himself would probably have said that it was due to the gallant leadership of his subordinate commanders, and the determination and vigour of all. The Corps Commander was extremely pleased with the work done and sent a special message of congratulation. We could indeed feel some satisfaction; the town was taken, a large amount of enemy equipment, including three more 88mm. guns and the 75mm. gun which had worried " D " Company, had also been captured, as well as a large haul of sugar. But the battle had cost us twenty-nine wounded, including Captain E. J. Benjafield, Lieutenant Compton and Lieutenant Sweeny, and six killed, including Major Elliot. The latter was a tremendous loss to his Company and to his Battalion. The last but one of the original key party called up in August, 1939, he was the epitome of the unit with his gay gallantry, quiet bravery and tremendous energy and efficiency.

While we remained with the Royal Scots in Goch, 46 and 227 Brigades were pushing southward on the other side of the Niers until, on the 21st February, they were held up a little forward of the railway from Goch to Udem. 44 Brigade was then sent across to continue the advance and capture the high ground some two thousand yards farther south, which dominated the road from Goch to Weeze. Three miles farther east, over the hill, lay Udem, still in enemy hands and well defended with guns which rained fierce fire on to the ground we had to take. The 6th Royal Scots Fusiliers had been put under command of 46 Brigade on the previous day and had had heavy casualties as they cleared the woods immediately south of the railway.

On the morning of the 23rd February, the attack began with the 6th K.O.S.B. on the right, and the 8th Royal Scots on the left, each with a squadron of Grenadiers. Again we followed the Royal Scots on to the start line, and as there was only one bridge over the small tributary of the Niers running through the woods, there was some delay in going through the bottleneck, so that we were a little late in crossing the start line. But the forward observation officers were able to continue the fire plan long enough to cover the leading Companies across the five hundred yards of open ground as far as the first objective. This was the two houses at Fasanenkath and the adjoining wood, which were taken by "D" and "B" Companies, respectively. Some prisoners of Battalion Graefing were found cowering in the houses, and two self-propelled guns were found in the garden, but the objective was taken with little difficulty, except from heavy shelling. The second objective was the big wood west of the road, which again could only be reached by crossing some six hundred yards of flat open ground, dominated by the enemy who held Host on the other side of the river. The second phase began at 1100 hours with "A" Company on the right and "C" Company on the left. After the heavy artillery concentration on the edge of the wood, the artillery observation post reported, "Prisoners of war coming back by the score," and on arrival there the Companies found that the enemy had not only abandoned excellent emplacements, which later withstood some very heavy enemy shelling, but also three more self-propelled guns. More were found on the east of the road by the Royal Scots. No further enemy were found until the southern edge of the wood was reached, but every yard of the advance was contested by shelling by guns of all calibres. This was made considerably worse by trees which gave them the effect of air-bursts. Soon after entering the wood Major Malone was killed by such a shell, and a moment later the stretcher bearer who went to his assistance was also killed. Major Malone had only joined the Battalion at Sevenum, after serving with the 50th Division, but he had immediately become a part of it, and his death was a sad blow to those who fought with him and had quickly learned to appreciate his quiet philosophy and humour. It was only by an amazing piece of luck that Company Sergeant-Major Overington did not become a casualty at the same time, as the second shell burst only a dozen feet from him. Though badly shaken, he rallied the Company Headquarters and handed over the Company to 2nd Lieutenant Buttery, who had recently joined the battalion and was fighting his first battle as a Platoon Commander. For the moment the shelling was confined to the north-west corner of the wood, so that "C" Company and the leading Platoons of "A" Company were able to move without harm. Lieutenant Gray's troop of Churchills, supporting "A" Company, pushed onwards under well nigh impossible conditions, and on the left Sergeant Beresford found he was unable to move his tanks through the woods and used the road instead. Never for a moment did the Guards allow the infantry to feel that they had lost that comforting support of the tanks should it become necessary to call for it. The far edge of the wood was reached by about 1530 hours. Both Companies took more prisoners, again from strongly built emplacements which they had to clear with grenades,

Beyond this they had not to go, and they could see enemy infantry and a self-propelled gun in the houses not 300 yards farther on between them and the road Weeze-Udem. Severe shelling continued all the time we occupied that position, and identifications of the 901st Panzer Grenadier Regiment and of the 741st German Headquarters Assault Gun Battalion indicated that there were considerably more in front of us than was expected. But Battalion Graefing, at any rate, was in a poor state and did not want to fight. A prisoner said that they had only come into the line the previous day and they had had a very severe pounding from our guns. All the same, there was a distinct possibility of a counter attack either from the south or from the east between the railway and the wood. Such an attack would hit the two Headquarters of the 6th K.O.S.B. and the 8th Royal Scots who were in the two houses at Fasanenkath, and cut off the Companies. " D " Company was moved to the north edge of the main wood, and a Company of the 6th Royal Scots Fusiliers took their place round the two Headquarters. Once the infantry were in position, a troop of 107 Anti-Tank Regiment moved up to the forward edge of the wood, and No. 2 Squadron Grenadier Guards moved to a forward rally behind Battalion Headquarters. Any movement of armour immediately brought down very heavy concentrations of artillery fire, but strangely enough they rarely hit the road, though Battalion Headquarters was often in the centre of one. In the position, wireless communications were very difficult owing to the trees, and lines were laid in an incredibly short time. Great praise is due to the Signallers for the way in which they maintained line communication to the Companies in spite of the heaviest shelling, and especially to Lieutenant Fullarton, attached to us from the Royal Signals, on the day before the attack on Blerick. He accompanied nearly every line party, and many were required before we left that area. For his great devotion to duty he was awarded the Military Cross. A word should also be said in acknowledgment of Sergeant Hunt's untiring efforts to keep touch by wireless, which had no small influence on events, as will be seen later.

The object of this operation was to seize the high ground overlooking the west side of the Niers, so that the 53rd Division could advance from Goch and capture Weeze. At last light, " A " Company sent a patrol to Heisehof and Vasenhof, after a preliminary bombardment, but it met no active opposition there. The area of Vasenhof was occupied by the dismounted Carrier Platoon under the command of Lieutenant Culbert. The Corps Commander was very anxious that we should dominate the road bridge over the stream south of Rottum, and this was the main task of the Carriers. However, they were unable to see the bridge owing to the " Bund " on the other side of the Niers, and it was agreed to dominate it by long range machine gun fire from more favourable positions farther north. The Carriers, however, remained at Vasenhof in a position to command Rottum. Their security depended a good deal on wireless communication, and any information they could give had to be passed back by this means. From where they were they could see everything that happened between Rottum and Weeze. The area from Rottum to Host was equally well observed by Captain Shaw, Royal Artillery, who established his observation post on the hillock known as " Mary," protected by two snipers, Privates Cowell and Darrant. His first success was to bring down a most effective concentration of mediums on four tanks as they retired from Host.

During the next day these two positions were to prove most valuable to the Welsh Division as they attacked southwards on either side of the road Goch-Weeze. In view of this attack, a very large " no firing " area in front of them had been prescribed to us. But our observation over the battlefield was so good that this could be dispensed with to a great extent, and the precaution was made almost unnecessary when it was found that, by some strange fortune, the leading tanks with the 53rd Division were operating on the same wireless frequency as our own rear link set to Brigade Headquarters. By 0715 hours the 6th Royal Welch Fusiliers could be seen fighting in Host, and as the battle raged the enemy began to give and straggle back to Rottum, ultimately to come within range of the Brens of the Carrier Platoon, who must have inflicted considerable casualties on them; and on to those who were out of range, they could easily direct the fire of the 3in. mortars with equal effect, so long as the wireless worked. It did. Throughout the day we took part in the Welsh Division's battle, being able to pass to their tanks exact information about pin-point targets and answering in return their requests for fire support. It was a Staff College battle come true, with no serious anxieties about one's own troops. Just after three o'clock the Carriers sent back details of enemy positions in Rottum, and reported that a staff car had just driven up to the village from the south. It was immediately engaged by the 3in. mortars who scored a direct hit. Major Jackson, who was thoroughly enjoying himself on the rear link, reported this at once. " Good," replied the G 3, Captain Glennie, " Was anyone inside ?"

" Too far to see," was the answer, " but we've made the ——— walk."

Soon afterwards the tanks reported that the enemy were withdrawing from Host and asked if we could engage. This was answered by an enthusiastic " Wilco." Major Graham, Royal Artillery, leapt into immediate action, and brought down devastating fire on the fleeing Germans. So the battle moved on. A short time after dark, the 71st Brigade continued the attack which rolled away beyond us. On the following evening we were relieved by the 3rd Division and went back to Turnhout for a rest and special training.

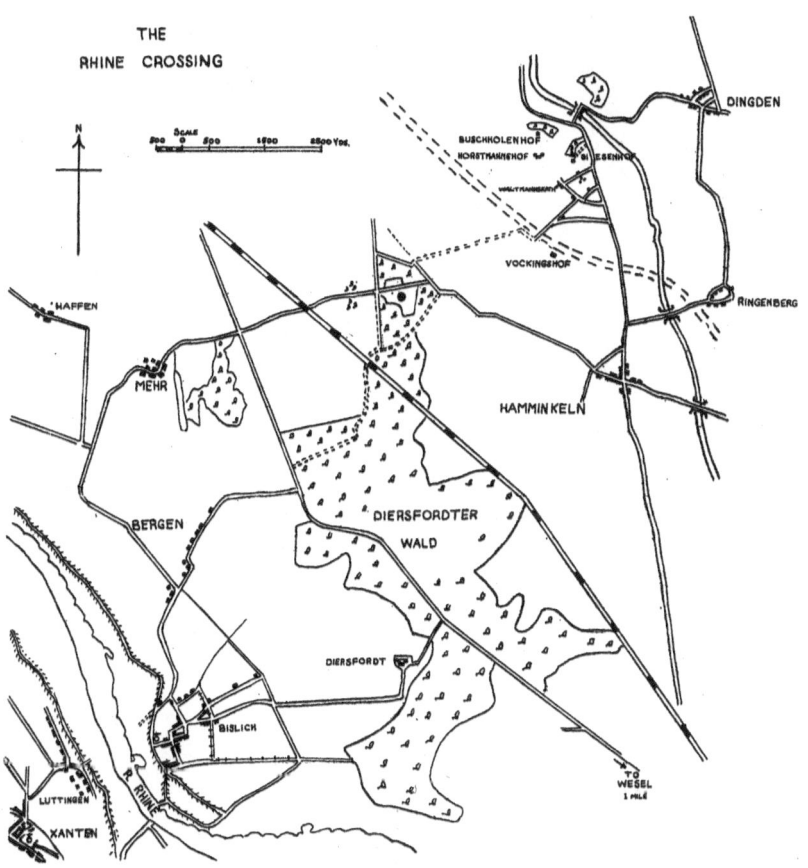

CHAPTER XIII.

The Rhine Crossing.

It was no surprise to anyone when the Division moved after a few days to the Diest area to do amphibious training. In fact, it was expected that the Scottish Division would do the Rhine crossing. We arrived in Zelem on the 6th March, and soon began to train for the new task. Wood clearing and the attack under smoke were the first tactical operations to be perfected, then came training with Buffaloes and stormboats, leading to a full scale Divisional crossing of the Maas near Maeseyck, first by day and then by night. This was the rehearsal for the Rhine crossing.

As the training drew to an end, reconnaissances were being made in the area selected for the attack. By a happy coincidence, our attack was to be made in that sector held by the 52nd (Lowland) Division, and during the preparatory period we were able to meet some old friends in the 4th and 5th Battalions. 44 Brigade was to make an assault crossing from the village of Luttingen, about a mile north of Xanten. This area was held by the 7/9th Royal Scots, and from the security of their observation post in the tower of the cathedral an excellent view could be obtained over the objective —the village of Bislich—and over the woods beyond. It might, however, be remarked that this ideal ground reconnaissance added nothing to the information we had already gleaned from up-to-date air photographs. It did confirm that a certain white house which appeared on the photographs as an important landmark on the Bund really did exist. But by the time the Battalion moved in great secrecy during the night of 22nd-23rd March to the area west of Xanten, nearly every commander had seen the ground over which he had to attack, and the general impression was that it was not as bad as it might be.

The 12th Corps was conducting this great operation, with the 1st Commando Brigade on the right, the 15th (Scottish) Division in the centre, and the 51st (Highland) Division on the left. It was to be done by night, and elaborate preparations were made to maintain security. For several nights before the operation, a considerable length of the west bank of the Rhine on either side of the actual crossing place was concealed by a huge smoke screen, behind which the troops concentrated. The Battalion arrived in Labbeck in the early hours of the 23rd March, and after breakfast went to bed after their long journey from Zelem, while the Company Commanders, who had come the night before, made final preparations. There they remained until dark, when they began to move along the taped tracks to the forward assembly area in Luttingen ready to cross.

The Divisional plan was for the 44th Brigade to seize Bislich and patrol as far as the woods beyond, while the 227th Brigade attacked farther north and made for Mehr. On each bank of the river a steep Bund, some twenty feet high, ran approximately parallel to the river, and between 200 and 300 yards from the water's edge. On the west side it was possible for the Royal Engineers to breach the Bund so that the Buffaloes could get down to the water. On the enemy side the Bund would have to be assaulted by infantry and a way on to it found for the vehicles after they had been unloaded. It was possible for the Buffaloes to go almost as far as the Bund before disgorging their cargoes, and from there a track ran to the top of the Bund near to the White House which had been noticed as a landmark. But before any carriers or anti-tank guns could get up, the Bund had to be cleared, and emplacements with wire could be seen from the observation posts. Mines, too, were expected. The Brigade plan, therefore, was to make the initial assault with the 6th Royal Scots Fusiliers on the right and the 8th Royal Scots on the left, each crossing in Buffaloes. The 6th K.O.S.B. would then follow the 6th Royal Scots Fusiliers and capture Bislich once the Royal Scots Fusiliers had seized and cleared the Bund. It was expected that the fight might well be hard, as considerable activity had been observed behind Bislich during the 23rd March, and troops had been seen debussing in full view. But we knew the details of many of the enemy positions and could lay down adequate preparatory fire on them, including a " stonk " on the top of the Bund and a " pepperpot " with Vickers machine guns and Bofors guns. These latter guns were also used to give directional fire on the left and right of the assault.

Shortly before 2300 hours on the 23rd March the Commando Brigade opened the attack about three miles farther up stream with the intention of capturing Wesel, and at 2304 hours they reported that they had got across with little opposition and were going well, having taken forty prisoners of the 1052nd Grenadier Regiment. Soon after this the Highland Division crossed and by midnight had elements of four battalions in Rees, having met little opposition except for mines. So the prospects were very encouraging. Meanwhile, in order to avoid casualties on the way to the forward artillery area from retaliatory shelling, the three Battalions of the Lowland Brigade had moved to Luttingen and were sheltering in the houses.

At 0155 hours on the 24th March the first wave of the assaulting Battalions began to cross in the Buffaloes of the 11th Royal Tanks, and by 0220 hours all the leading Companies were across. Corporal Dyson and Private Day went across with them with the express object of finding the White House and placing a lamp there so that no one would miss this vital point in the darkness. It was not long before the 6th Royal Scots Fusiliers reported schu mines on the right of their sector, so, when our leading Company went over, Lieutenant Smith and some Pioneers were sent with them to sweep the top of the Bund and make it fit for us to use. No sooner had they reached the top and begun to sweep than a party of sixteen Germans came rushing across and surrendered to the surprised Pioneers. But quite apart from the exhilaration of having taken the first prisoners, they were very pleased to receive this very practical demonstration that the track was clear of mines. Soon after 0300 hours the Fusiliers reported that the Bund was taken, and a few minutes before four o'clock " A " and " B " Companies crossed in storm boats, followed as soon as possible by " C " and " D " Companies. One of the main essentials of this operation was an absolutely reliable system of communication from the forward Companies through Battalion Headquarters to Brigade. Each Company had its normal 18 set, but it was feared that when operating in the village there would be some screening which might cause them to lose touch with Battalion Headquarters, and past experience had always proved that a battle was much more efficiently controlled from a headquarters established near the start line and remaining there until some degree of stability had been achieved by the attacking Companies, With them also were the forward observation officers with their independent wireless links, but since they were crossing in storm boats with the infantry, they too had 18 sets. It was therefore decided that Captain Moffat should cross at the same time as " C " and " D " Companies and establish a forward Headquarters with an 18 set and a spare 22 set. Tactical Headquarters would then cross when this forward Headquarters had made contact with the Companies and Brigade, thus ensuring continuity of communications. Tactical Headquarters at this time was established in the cellar of a house just behind the Bund at Luttingen, and during a lull in the activities the Intelligence Officer surfaced to find the thatched roof and upper storeys of the house ablaze—much to the consternation of Major Graham, Royal Artillery, who, being rather anxious about communications, had come to the battle with more wireless sets than anyone had ever before seen on a carrier, and had established himself in the same cellar. So the very contingency we had planned to avoid was forced upon us, and we had to wander among the ruined houses in search of a command post while the battle was in progress. Eventually we came to rest in the remains of the ground floor room of a house with little wall and no roof, the cellar being full of troops waiting to cross !

By 0700 hours " A " Company, with No. 10 Platoon of " B " Company under command, had captured the centre and right of

Bislich, and the other two Platoons of "B" Company had cleared the left side of the village. There was some opposition by No. 1062 Grenadier Regiment, but it was not very serious. "C" and "D" Companies then went through "A" and "B" Companies, capturing their objectives just before ten o'clock.

It was most important that these forward Companies should get established by this time. In the order for operation "Torchlight," it had been stated that six hours after the zero hour of the 15th Division, No. 1 Airborne Corps would land in front of us and of the Commandos at Wesel. A minute or two before 1000 hours the cry went round, "They're here," and all eyes were turned to the west and north-west, where, glittering in the bright sunshine, were what looked like hundreds of big four-engined bombers, Dakotas and gliders. Over they went with a steady, conquering roar, and at exactly 1000 hours the parachutists began to drop over the Diersfordter Wald ahead—enthusiastically cheered by many of the Jocks on the ground. It was a wonderful and inspiring sight. The noise brought the civilians, who had been confined to certain houses, to the windows and doors to peer at the great armada, and even they could scarce forbear to cheer. Some in fact did, probably thinking that the Luftwaffe had arrived! The next thing to do was to get in touch with the airborne troops as soon as possible. We had been given a special wireless set for the purpose, and perched up in the roof of one of the houses, so as to get the best reception, Lieutenant Fullarton and Private Gray worked away ceaselessly with the set until at 1230 hours they were rewarded. They had got through and triumphantly brought the message that the airborne reported all objectives taken and everything going well.

While reorganising on their objective, "C" Company noticed a number of Germans retreating about six hundred yards in front of them, and as the mortars were at the time out of range, they engaged them with what weapons they had. Again at about 1215 hours the same thing occurred just after a patrol, consisting of Lieutenant Palmer and Corporal Macari, had been sent by the Company to make contact with the parachutists. Captain Carey and Company Sergeant-Major Millar immediately set off in the carrier "Chisholm" to round up the Germans. They overtook the patrol and successfully dealt with the Germans. Lieutenant Palmer and Corporal Macari caught up with the carrier, jumped aboard, and all set off to the corner of the wood which was the rendezvous. All the way they kept finding enemy stragglers who were "put in the bag." But more continued to appear on the flank, so, in order to prevent delay, Company Sergeant-Major Millar went off to get them while the carrier went on. Soon, movement was seen in the wood, and not wanting to risk the carrier being hit by a bazooka, Captain Carey went forward on foot. At

1345 hours, about one hundred yards from the pre-arranged meeting place, two American parachutists appeared out of a fox-hole—the link-up with the 17th American Airborne Division had been made.

It had been a wonderful day, and when in the evening the Battalion concentrated in Bergen ready to push through the Airborne Division on the following day, everybody was still marvelling at the events, a little bewildered by what was probably the most curious battle in which we had ever taken part. Less than twenty-four hours previously, a great river obstacle, the most formidable barrier to entrance into Germany, lay before us. It had been crossed with little trouble, beyond some shelling of Bislich, and only twelve casualties had been suffered. At 1000 hours we had gone out of the battle like a snap of the fingers, the shelling had ceased suddenly, for the parachutists had landed in the gun area, and after their arrival there had been little to do except collect weapons and ammunition and drive back, in a constant stream, the 274 dispirited Germans who were only too ready to give up the struggle. Of equipment there was any amount, including a 20mm. gun, four 75mm. guns, and numerous mortars and light machine guns of various types.

Next morning our task was to push north-eastward through the 6th Airborne Division to try to seize the bridge over the River Issel, west of Dingden. It was an advance to contact, with the 6th K.O.S.B. leading. For this operation we had under command the Sharpshooters from the 4th Armoured Brigade. Our route was to be via the cross roads where the road from Wesel crossed the road between Mehr and Hamminkeln, but this road was not open as 46 Brigade had not got as far as had been hoped, and the woods on the west side were held by enemy. So we used a track through the Diersfordter Wald. This was not a bad track, but was rather dangerous as enemy shelling had set fire to the undergrowth and ammunition was exploding near to it, and the smoke was dense and choking in places.

"A" Company was vanguard with one troop of self-propelled anti-tank guns, a section of 3-in. mortars, one section of our own anti-tank guns, a Platoon of machine guns, and Captain Meredith as forward observation officer. They were followed by "B" Company, Tactical Headquarters, "C" and "D" Companies. "A" and "B" Companies both rode on tanks, while "C" and "D" Companies followed on foot. The leading three tanks did not carry infantry so that they could come into immediate action when required. They were followed by No. 7 Platoon under Lieutenant Riley, Company Headquarters, No. 9 Platoon commanded by Sergeant Holloway, and No. 8 Platoon commanded by Lieutenant Spragg. As soon as No. 7 Platoon reached the railway line they came under machine gun fire from the wood in front of them on the right of the road.

Major Pallot immediately sent this Platoon to clear the wood, with covering fire from the tanks who fired into the wood ahead of them from positions on the left of the road near to the railway line. Enemy shelling at the level crossing was more intense than any we had met for a very considerable time, and Lieutenant Fullarton, who was there at the time attending to his wireless sets, stayed to do some very useful work as traffic control. Soon, however, No. 7 Platoon had cleared the wood, where a certain amount of enemy transport was captured, an airborne gun retrieved, and a beautiful pair of binoculars mounted on a tripod found. These were duly presented to the forward observation officer.

While waiting for this little battle to finish, Sergeant Hodges, who was acting Company Sergeant-Major, heard some German voices a short distance off the axis near to his Company headquarters. Taking a section of No. 9 Platoon, he carried out a private war of his own, assaulting the weapon slits and capturing 14 enemy.

The next trouble arose on the left flank, where the self-propelled anti-tank gunners reported enemy tanks beyond the railway line. North of the level crossing the road ran along the west side of No. 7 Platoon's wood, and was quite open to the enemy tanks. By 1125 hours, however, an advance had been made almost to the main road, when the leading Platoon again came under fire, and enemy were seen in the two small woods 250 yards to the left and on the main road. After an artillery concentration, No. 9 Platoon attacked with tank support, and by 1145 hours the Company objective was taken.

Owing to the necessity of taking the bridge quickly, it was decided to push on and not get the 8th Royal Scots, who were to have come up on the left, involved in a battle. It was not possible to use this exposed axis in daylight, but a track was found through the wood to the main road some fifteen hundred yards from the autobahn. At this point the woods crossed the main road, and a small road branched north-eastward to the autobahn. By 1600 hours all the Companies were in the area, with the 6th Royal Scots Fusiliers picketting the Brigade axis behind. But the minor road passed across absolutely open country, and it was quite impossible to cross it in daylight as it was dominated by self-propelled guns which had already immobilised three tanks.

Just before orders for the attack were given by the Commanding Officer at " D " Company's Headquarters, information was received that the 116th Panzer Division had reappeared on the other side of the Issel, south-east of us, making the need for urgency more acute. The line of the autobahn could probably be gained with some ease, but the country beyond was dotted with farms, and it was decided to do a silent attack as soon after dark as possible. Companies would successively bite their way forward until " B "

Company could reach a position from which "D" Company could launch an assault on the bridge.

As soon as it was dark enough to move across the open, the Carriers dashed forward and seized what the next day's newspapers described as the "important motor road." On arrival, however, it was found to be nothing but the foundations of an autobahn, and even the Carriers stuck in the sand! At 2000 hours "D" Company crossed the autobahn and seized the first group of farm buildings, silently and with no trouble. "C" Company went through them to Waltmannskath, while Battalion Headquarters established itself at Vockingshof. So far, no opposition had been met. When "A" Company went through "C" Company to the next farm, they met some enemy and had to fight for their objective. They captured it after a short engagement, but surprise had been lost. However, "B" Company took the next objective, Giesenhof, with little trouble. As the secret was broken, it was decided to postpone the assault on the bridge so that the enemy might settle down again, and some degree of surprise regained.

Meanwhile, Corporal Guthrie and Private Yates, of "D" Company, patrolled forward to try to discover the state of the bridge, but at every place where they attempted to cross the road they found enemy. Prisoners captured by "A" Company had already reported some forty paratroops farther east with five guns, and now enemy infantry and probably self-propelled guns were reported in the area of Buschholenhof, on "B" Company's left. "C" Company were, therefore, despatched to seize this place just before "D" Company began to move forward through "B" Company, ready for their assault at 0430 hours. Lieutenant MacDonald's Platoon took the first buildings of the farm, in fact the enemy appeared to allow them to get in, but as the next Platoon moved round to capture the remainder, a savage counter attack of about battalion strength broke upon "C" and "B" Companies while "D" Company was moving through "B" Company's position. By an ill-chance, Battalion Headquarters was also moving at the time. Owing to bad communications, which was largely due to interference by a persistent American voice and a B.B.C. crooner singing "I can't give you anything but love," the Commanding Officer decided to move Headquarters up to "B" Company's area, and was actually crossing the autobahn when the counter attack began. It was the one and only time during the campaign that the Battalion was really caught unbalanced. Captain Moffat, who had gone forward in the dingo scout car to see what was happening, was at the time at "B" Company's Headquarters, when a large number of enemy, apparently drunk, appeared in the half light of the searchlights. Thinking they were wanting to surrender, Lieutenant Milne, of "D" Company, jumped into the dingo, and ordered Private Featherstone, the driver, to drive towards them while he stood up shouting to them to give up. Covered by our Bren guns, they managed to drive through the foremost enemy who were too surprised to react to this extraordinary action, but when the Germans recovered from their initial amazement, they opened up with machine guns, and Lieutenant Milne was killed. There was no retreat for Private Featherstone, so with great presence of mind he drove on as fast as he could, swung left, and eventually escaped round the back of the enemy.

Meanwhile, " D " Company had managed to disengage and had had got into position, but " C " Company, almost surrounded, and with no positions to go to, fought fiercely until all their rounds and grenades were spent and then retired. Lieutenant MacDonald was able to get the majority of his Platoon away under cover of the Brens, but Lance-Corporal Avory, Private Spalding, and Private Webster, who manned them to the end, were captured. While this battle was in progress the barn in which the wounded had been collected was hit by a bazooka and set on fire. Lance-Corporal Brooks and Private Rudkin did magnificent work as stretcher bearers, but they were unable to get all the wounded before Private Rudkin was captured with those who remained.

Farther to the right the attack had run against No. 12 Platoon's position on the edge of the orchard. Against this, the attack eventually broke after a bitter action. Private Howe, who was manning the Bren gun in the corner, inflicted tremendous casualties on the oncoming enemy until his gun jammed. Then coolly fetching another, he resumed fire until he was killed at his post and his section wiped out. In the morning this section was found dead in their positions with Private Howe's lifeless fingers still grasping his gun. They had given all, and had broken the counter attack. Ninety-eight German dead were found round that Platoon's position. By 0630 hours the situation was completely in hand, though " C " Company, in retiring from Buschholenhof, had found a strong enemy post at Horstmannshof. The Commanding Officer therefore went to " B " Company and planned an attack on this place with Major Tinniswood. No. 11 Platoon, commanded by Lieutenant Allard, attacked at first light; but the enemy, who had been so confident and aggressive during the night, were in no shape to fight in the morning, and one hundred and thirty two prisoners quickly surrendered. The wounded left by " C " Company were freed, the Germans having left them with Private Rudkin in charge. So the situation was restored, but the action had cost one officer and seventy casualties, mainly from " C " Company.

The rapid advance during the previous day had brought 44 Brigade into the rear of the 7th Parachute Division, and across its lines of communication. The 8th Royal Scots, who had come up on our left, were continually attacked, and prisoners said that the Battalion which had attacked us during the night had been hurried from Bocholt specially to stop our advance through the enemy's rear areas. About mid-day ten tanks appeared north of us, but were driven off by all available guns. Later in the afternoon the 6th Royal Scots Fusiliers, having found that the bridge was blown, assaulted the River Issel in daylight, and by 1700 hours had three companies across. But opposition was tough and there was a good deal of shelling on them and us. " D " Company, under Major Smith, had spread across the main road in front of " A " Company, but farther south some enemy still remained between them and Hamminkeln. They were not particularly aggressive, but they could not be approached across the open ground swept as it was by 88s and machine guns over the river. A complication now arose in the shape of a heavy thunderstorm, and drenching rain made the tracks through our positions quite impassable to the heavy bridging column. The only alternative route was along the main road from Hamminkeln. Shortly before midnight we were ordered to send a patrol along this road to meet the bridging train north of Hamminkeln. The Carriers were detailed for this vital patrol and set off cautiously towards the rendezvous. The enemy on the road were overwhelmed, and at last, at 0225 hours on the 26th March, the message came over the wireless that they had made contact with the sappers. The column roared up the road with a Bren gunner on the roof of each lorry, and by 0600 hours the bridge was in position.

Gradually, the 6th Royal Scots Fusiliers strengthened their positions in spite of heavy shelling which we also shared; but they had continuous casualties, and towards evening a heavy counter attack developed. " A " and " D " Companies were ordered across the river to assist them, but the attack was beaten off and was not repeated. Later in the night, the 53rd Division attacked northwards, east of the river. By 0400 hours they were in Dingden, and the Lowland Brigade's task was completed.

CHAPTER XIV.

THE CHASE THROUGH GERMANY.

EVENTS were now moving so fast that only the movements of Corps and Armies were of interest to those not in contact with the enemy. By the 3rd April the Armour had swept beyond Munster towards Bremen, Hamburg and Brauschweig, while the Airborne Division and the 6th Guards Tank Brigade with an American Airborne Division were driving rapidly due east. It was time that the Scottish Division caught up with the battle after its rest, and on the 5th April the Lowland Brigade moved to an area some fifteen miles north-west of Munster, and harboured at Borghorst. Two days later the advance was continued through Greven, across the River Ems through Lengerich and Osnabrock to the small village of Schmalge, about six miles north of Lubbecke and fourteen north-west of Minden. It was unfortunate that it was not possible to look at the famous battlefield, but woods had to be cleared in the neighbourhood. The general situation at the time was that the Americans had crossed the River Weser and were on the high ground between Obernkirchen and Rodenberg, and had reached a point only ten miles south of Hanover. The 6th Airborne Division were fifteen miles west of that city with the 15th Reconnaissance Regiment, who were working with them securely in possession of the bridge over the River Leine at Neustadt. Farther left the 11th Armoured Division were up to the Weser, and the 7th Armoured Division were ten miles from Bremen.

On the 10th april the Battalion crossed the Weser at Petershagen to stay the night at the German hutted camp at Loccum, going on to Gailhof, about ten miles north of Hanover on the following day. During the night of the 11th-12th April, 46 Brigade and 227 Brigade crossed the Fusche Canal and attacked Celle from the south-west and west, respectively, and by daylight 227 Brigade had crossed the River Aller running through the town. West of Celle, however, Forst Fuhrberg was not cleared, and during the afternoon of the 12th April the 6th K.O.S.B. was in process of clearing this great wood. But while this was being done, negotiations were in progress with the local German commander concerning 50,000 political prisoners in a camp nearby—a camp in which there was a serious epidemic of typhus. This was the notorious Belsen camp. At 1658 hours a message was received saying that, as a result of the negotiations, the enemy were to evacuate the wooded area west of the River Ortze, which joined the Aller due north of the wood, and

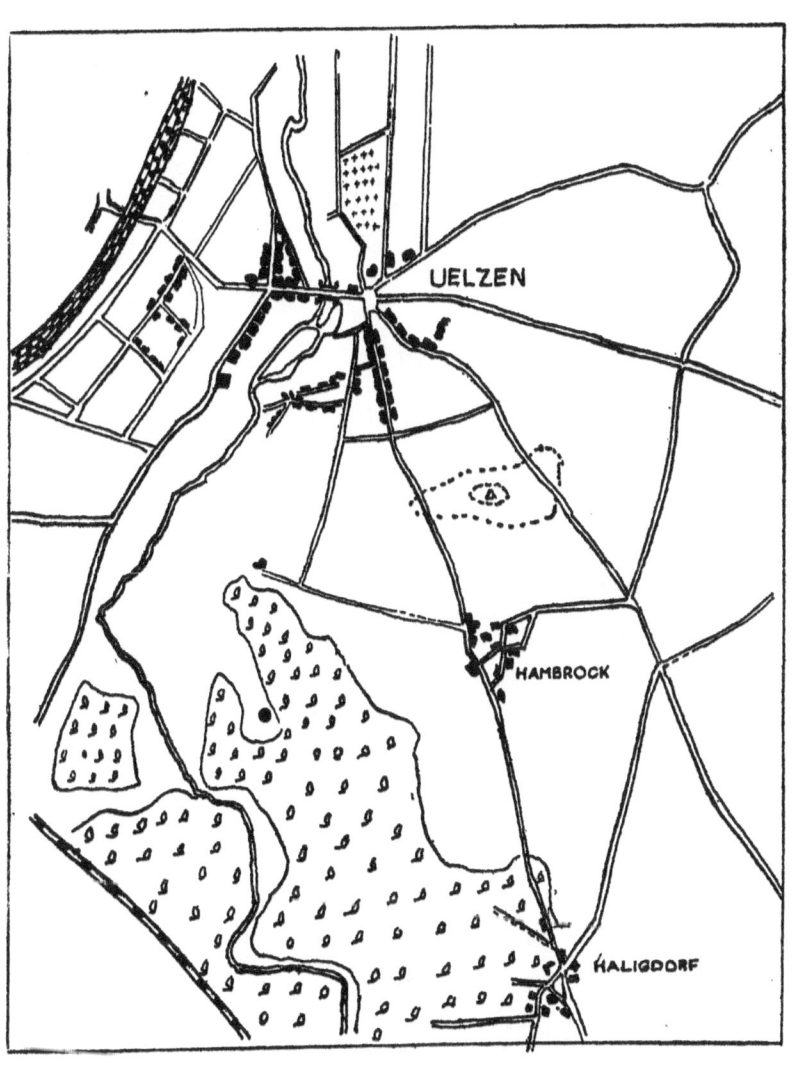

for approximately five miles north of the Aller. The 6th K.O.S.B., therefore, were told to keep off the road Hambuhren-Steinforde. At 1940 hours " A " Company was sent to Hambuhren, and Major Pallot fired the two red Verey lights, which was the signal for the evacuation to be put in motion.

The Battalion then settled into Celle airfield, and after a Regimental Sergeant-Major's parade, moved on the following afternoon to the Gas School in the north-east part of Celle. Around here, 44 Brigade concentrated preparatory to following 227 Brigade to a further concentration area near Uelzen. By 0645 hours on the 14th April the 10th Highland Light Infantry, of that Brigade, was fighting in the outskirts of the town. 44 Brigade followed up on the axis Celle-Eschede-Weyhausen-Uelzen, with 46 Brigade on the right, moving along the road south of the Forst Sprakensehl. Progress was considerably handicapped by felled trees and demolitions. The 6th K.O.S.B. were acting as advance guard and eventually were held up by one such demolition. The Commanding Officer went forward to see Major Twogood, and almost immediately up drove the Brigadier. " You'd better build a bridge," said the Brigadier. " Maurice," said the Colonel, " you'd better build a bridge." Turning to Lieutenant Cockburn, the Company Commander repeated, " Norman, build a bridge." Seeing his Platoon Sergeant nearby, the Platoon Commander said, " Get a bridge built, Sergeant." And with the speed of lightning, the order had passed from the Brigade Commander to a handful of unfortunate private soldiers who immediately began to look around for materials with which to perform this formidable task!

At 1230 hours, the harbour parties, as usual led by Captain Elder, but this time with an escorting Platoon of " B " Company, went to reconnoitre the area of Rabe, a small village north-west of the main axis. On approaching the village they found that it had not been cleared and proceeded to do the work, capturing about forty prisoners including some who had been discharged from the army on the previous day! The rot was apparently setting in.

As 227 Brigade were not able to capture Uelzen owing to stiff resistance, 44 Brigade was ordered to do a flanking movement round the right to open an axis for the Airborne Division. The author is unable to give a first-hand account of the ensuing actions, but is, fortunately, able to quote the following description written by Lieut.-Colonel Richardson :—

" On the 15th April 44 Brigade was ordered to capture a series of villages held by the enemy with a view to closing on the eastern half of Uelzen, through which the Rivar Ilmenau flows. One squadron of Coldstream Guards was placed under command for this operation. The villages concerned were Wrestedt, Haligsdorf and Hambrock, and those were allotted to the 8th Royal Scots, the 6th Royal Scots Fulsiliers and the 6th K.O.S.B., respectively. With the capture of Hambrock, a firm base some six hundred yards from Uezlen would be secured.

" Little opposition was encountered by the 8th Royal Scots, but the Fusiliers found Haligsdorf held, and considerable fighting took place. Moreover, efforts to proceed along the main road to Hambrock were strongly contested. Mortar fire was not heavy but was continuous. On the capture of Neindorf and Haligdorf, the 6th K.O.S.B. entered the latter village and from there launched their attack on Hambrock. The Commanding Officer's plan was to by-pass Haligsdorf on the west and advance through the woods until level with Hambrock, then using one Company as a firm base, to take Hambrock from the west. Another Company would then be passed through to dominate Uelzen and secure the left flank.

" " B " Company, commanded by Major Tinniswood, M.C. led the advance and established itself in such a position as to dominate Hambrock, but not without casualties, since the enemy in the village were extremely lively and possessed a number of 20mm. guns. Lieutenant Riley was wounded at this point. To " D " Company fell the execution of the assault, and indeed it appeared a formidable task since a stretch of four hundred yards of completely open ground had to be crossed, and it was obvious that the Bosche were in fighting mood. However, Hambrock was subjected to a short but intense artillery and mortar bombardment, after which every possible weapon laid down smoke, and the Company, with No. 17 Platoon commanded by Sergeant O'Neal, and No. 18 Platoon commanded by Sergeant Snowball, leading, charged across the open. This dashing and gallant attack was too much for the Bosche who, after some brisk exchanges, gave in, leaving sixty-three prisoners and no less than eight 20mm. guns in the Company's hands.

" This affray was one of the best Company exploits of the whole campaign and was typical of the Battalion's morale at the time. " D " Company were immensely elated by their success, and particular mention must be made of No. 17 Platoon who exhibited a drive which no enemy could resist. Sergeant O'Neal was subsequently awarded a well merited Military Medal, and other men to distinguish themselves were Corporal Williams, and Private Brown who was in command of the 2 in. mortar.

" Later in the evening " C " Company, commanded by Major Twogood, pushed through " B " Company, dug in and secured the left flank. Battalion Headquarters and " A " Company moved to Haligsdorf, and so ended a successful day.

"The 16th April was a beautiful summer-like day and was spent in improving Company positions and exchanging shots with the enemy in the southern outskirts of Uelzen. It was a good day for snipers, and Sergeant Stoddart killed a German stone dead at six hundred yards and " winged " another. The Commanding Officer visited all Companies, finding them tremendously enthusiastic. The 6th Royal Scots Fusiliers pushed out to the east, and with 46 Brigade in contact with the enemy on the west of the town, the time for the assault on Uelzen was ripe. The Divisional plan was to assault Uelzen with 44 Brigade on the right and 46 Brigade on the left on the night of the 17th-18th April, but before this matured the Borderers were to have a considerable say in affairs, and effect on the operations in general.

" Once again a perfect summer's day broke on the 17th April, a day likely to linger long in the memory of those who took part in the events. 44 Brigade was to attack with the 6th Royal Scots Fusiliers on the right and the 6th K.O.S.B. on the left, but the activities of the Battalion were to have a very great bearing on the battle long before zero hour arrived. Let it again be emphasised that the Germans in Uelzen were in fighting mood, and efforts to gain an easy success by the other Brigades had met with stubborn resistance. The southeast part of the town was firmly held, and it was here that Sergeant Stoddart made his remarkable kill the previous day.

" Lieutenant-Colonel Richardson was in Hambrock at an early hour and was conducted to a grand-stand seat on the northern edge by Captain MacNab. Across the open ground, the Germans in position south of the houses could clearly be seen. The Commanding Officer was anxious to test the strength of the enemy here, to determine whether it would be a preliminary and separate attack that night, or whether the positions could be swept up in the general advance. Accordingly, he ordered two sections of the Carrier Platoon to advance cautiously along the roads from Hambrock and from the cross-roads east of that village, covered by a Platoon of " D " Company on the northern edge of Hambrock.

" Sergeant ' Crasher ' White, of Jedburgh, commanded the section on the left road, and Corporal Rutland, of Keswick, commanded that on the right. They started at 0900 hours, covered by the Platoon of " D " Company who were delighted to expend some ammunition. It was with something approaching horror that the spectators saw Sergeant White's carriers in full cry down the road and dart into the enemy's position. The Bosche were completely taken aback by this bold and unorthodox action, early resisters were shot by the crew of the leading carrier, and white flags began to appear. The section under Corporal Rutland was very quick to appreciate the situation and rapidly closed on the eastern part of the objective. The carriers mopped up rapidly and secured a foothold.

"The Commanding Officer now realised that a great chance of exploiting success presented itself, and accordingly orders were despatched for " D " Company to move at once to Uelzen and exploit the carriers' gains, and for " A " and " B " Companies to move into Hambrock; Battalion Headquarters was also summoned. All Companies moved with commendable speed, the men thoroughly entering into what they knew to be an impromptu operation. " D " Company poured into Uelzen and began a northward drive, while " B " Company was ordered to relieve the carriers on the southern edge and form a firm base.

"Things were not, however, to go entirely in our favour. Germans in the houses on the river bank assisted their comrades, and a self-propelled gun accompanied by about fifty riflemen launched a counter attack from the cross roads, and for some minutes things looked extremely unpleasant. This self-propelled gun was very boldly handled, and knocked out two carriers which were empty except for the signaller, Private Campbell, who bravely manned his set until he was killed, and fired into two houses held by " D " Company, whose No. 17 Platoon, emboldened by their brilliant success on the 15th April, had let enthusiasm over-ride discretion and had gone too far forward. Sergeant O'Neal made a most gallant attempt to destroy this self-propelled gun with a Piat, but was betrayed at the last moment by a civilian. However, the Bosch infantry were not up to their task, and gradually the Borderers gained the upper hand and continued to advance. " A " Company now launched a gallant attack across the open to clear the enemy from the houses on the river bank after which the enemy's enthusiasm visibly declined, and by 1800 hours the Commanding Officer was able to report to the Brigadier that half the Brigade's objective for the night had been captured.

"Much hard fighting took place during this impromptu battle which had a very great effect on subsequent operations, and which was accorded a special mention in the 8th Corps Order of the Day.

"The success must be attributed to the energy, determination and initiative of Sergeant White and his Carrier Section, and the award of the Military Medal for this exploit was a fitting reward. " A," " B," and " D " Companies seconded his efforts splendidly. During the evening General Barber, who had come forward to congratulate the Battalion, asked the Commanding Officer to try to capture the important bridge over the Ilmenau in the centre of the town. This was covered by the enemy at close range both by small arms and by a self-propelled gun, but in its present mood the Battalion was equal to the task, and No. 7 Platoon, commanded by

Sergeant Lee, stormed it, overpowered the guards, and established a precarious bridgehead which they maintained until the end of the operation.

" The Brigade attack was launched at 0400 hours on the 18th April, and was so successful that the whole objective was in our hands by 0700 hours. Battalion Headquarters was established in a luxurious hotel. " B " Company had to bear with a cemetery!

" Although snipers were troublesome the Battalion had an interesting day looking across the river and watching 46 Brigade clearing their part of the objective, which they did not complete until 1900 hours. An amusing incident took place when a Platoon of " B " Company observed a member of the Wehrmacht seek a secluded spot and commence his daily duty. At a given signal, Brens, rifles and the 2 in. mortar opened rapid fire, whereupon the German departed like a rabbit leaving his trousers behind, to the vast enjoyment of the Borderers."

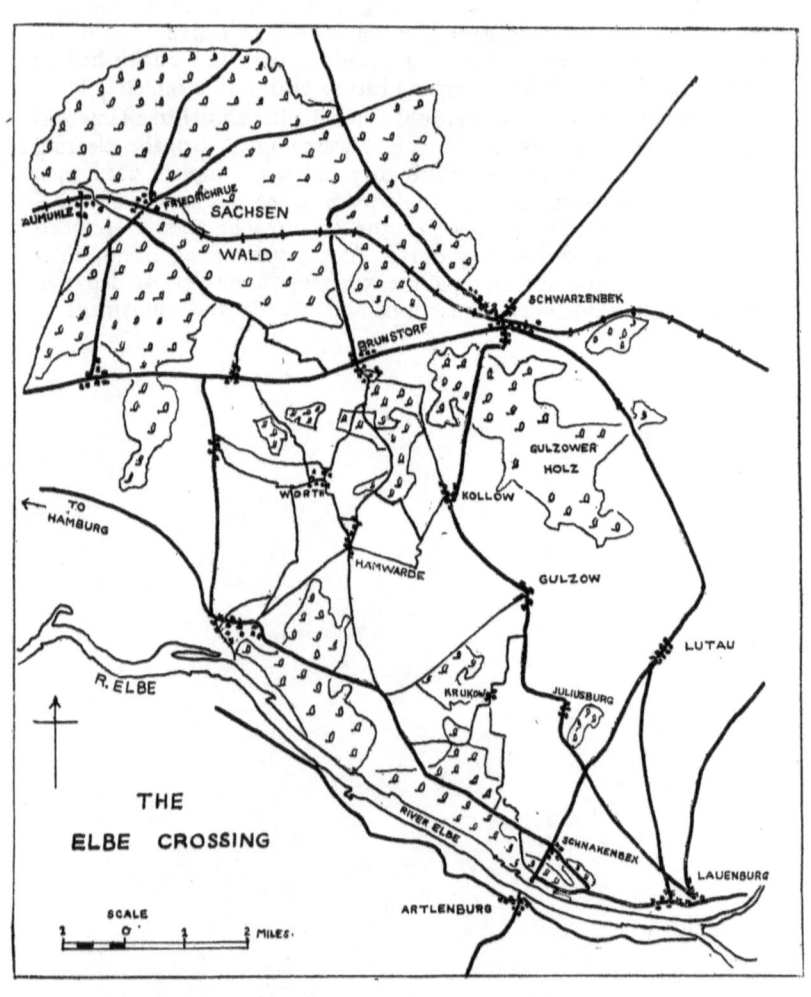

CHAPTER XV.

The Elbe.

Since Uelzen, the whole attitude of everyone had changed again; this time from a burning desire to achieve the victory which was so obviously ahead, to an attitude of wondering whether victory would come before the Battalion could do any more. In front of us was another great obstacle—the Elbe, the river which in so many minds divides eastern Germany from the west. Would we have to cross it? If anyone had to do so, we were almost certain that it would be the Scottish Division. But there were astonishing rumours of Russian progress. Was the Elbe to be the boundary between the British and the Russian armies? Even if that were not the plan, would the Soviet army reach the river first? Perhaps they would, and we should not be needed to make an assault crossing. River crossings are hazardous, uncertain operations, and no one looks forward to them with quite the same confidence as to a dry operation; and perhaps there were some who would not have been sorry to have been told that an assault crossing would not be necessary. Yet everybody knew in the back of his mind that the next operation was the crossing of the Elbe, and that it would be just as successful as the crossing of the Rhine.

Then again there were numerous questions and answers about the state of the enemy on the other side. That he was demoralised and beaten, everyone knew. Would he make a desperate, all-out effort to hold the great western barrier of his inner fortress, while he brought the army in Norway across in a forlorn attempt to win back Berlin? It was already known that the 264th Infantry Division had been moved from Denmark to Lubeck. There was a rumour that Himmler himself was commanding the battle from his headquarters at Schwarzenbeck some fifteen miles beyond the river, and he was said to have surrounded himself with loyal and desperate S.S. troops who would probably resist fircely in the wooded area round that town.

The atmosphere was tense with such speculations, rumours and hopes. But the planners quietly set themselves to the task of planning the final blow which was to bring to an end hostilities in the west. Details of the enemy dispositions east of the Elbe were not known, but it was appreciated that the line of the river from Lauenburg to Geestacht was held by little more than two battalions, excluding anti-aircraft troops and some odd police units. It was also known with some certainty that the Artle· burg ferry was defended by a company, while something like a hundred guns of varying calibres covered the area from the line of the railway running through Schwarzenbek. Little of the defences were shown on the air photographs. As usual, a very clear impression of the terrain could be obtained from them, but even the air camera could not pierce the dense pine woods which stretched almost to the water's edge between Lauenburg and Geesthacht.

This was the place selected for the attack of the Scottish Division. The 1st Commando Brigade, which was under command for this operation " Enterprise," was to attack Lauenburg. On the left the Lowland Brigade was to attack from Artlenburg astride the ferry and capture the eastern part of the woods and the village of Schnakenbek beyond. It was apparent that the woods were very thick and that the main exit from the river bank to Schnakenbek was narrow, closely flanked by steep wooded banks, and it was a reasonable deduction that this defile would be held and accurately registered. A further difficulty was the steepness of the cliffs on the east side of this exit where the Battalion would have to land. An excellent oblique photograph showed more clearly the nature of this obstacle. It was the sheer face of a quarry from which the only exit westward was the road through the woods to Schakenbek, and eastwards a questionable track at the end of the quarry which might be negotiated by agile infantry only. Even when the infantry had reached the top, there was no easy way to the village, and, if the defile was to be avoided, the choice was between an advance along the cliff for one thousand yards and then round a hairpin bend along the road to Schnakenbek, half of which road would not have been cleared by the assaulting Battalion, and a very doubtful track through the woods, which, if adequate, was more direct. The latter course was preferred, and the Intelligence Officer was sent up in an air observation post to find out whether the plan was feasible. When he went up the bright spring sun had drawn up a faint mist which softened even the white glare of the quarry face. The four hundred yard wide river flowed quietly with a moderate current, and the hard beaches on the foreshore of the quarry promised a good landing. An air of sleepy peace was over the whole wide scene. Not a movement of any sort could be seen.

Lieutenant-Colonel Richardson, therefore, decided that after the assaulting Battalions had landed and taken their objectives, the 6th Royal Scots Fusiliers east of the ferry, the 8th Royal Scots on the west, " C " Company under Major Twogood should cross in Buffaloes, form up in the quarry, negotiate the track out of the eastern end and go through the wood to take the south-eastern corner of Schnakenbek. " A " and " B " Companies, under Major Pallot and

Major Tinniswood, M.C., would then go through to take the middle of the village, and " D " Company, under Major Smith, would follow to secure the northern exit of the village. Two companies of the 2nd Argyll and Sutherland Highlanders would then take over and expand " C " Company's area, while " C " Company moved westwards along the edge of the wood to an objective on the west side of the road from the ferry. This road would thus be secured for the anti-tank guns and vehicles to use as soon as they could be landed. When the village had been taken, the Carrier Platoon, with or without carriers, according to whether or not they had been landed, would seize a knoll about six hundred yards north-east of the village.

Operation " Enterprise " was made a replica of operation " Torchlight " as far as possible in the planning stage, and this was all complete on the 28th April. Unfortunately, the Commanding Officer fell sick on that day, and Major Jackson commanded the Battalion, with Captain Moffat acting as Second-in-Command. In the evening of that day the Battalion moved out of Luneburg to a large wood near Brietlingen, and about seven miles short of Artlenburg. Here we rested, fed and made final preparations before boarding the Buffaloes of the 11th Royal Tanks. The leading Battalions crossed at 0200 hours on the 29th April and met little opposition except light mortaring at regular intervals. The 6th K.O.S.B., also in Buffaloes, crossed an hour and a half after the leading Battalions. By this time the enemy had got the range of the crossing and was shelling accurately. But the Battalion got across without casualties, largely because the landing discipline was good and there was no bunching. Two Companies of the Argylls who crossed at the same time were unlucky, as a salvo landed in the quarry at the moment they disembarked, with the result that they had several casualties—a sickening sight for our troops as they came to the shore a few minutes later. By 0500 hours " C " Company were on their objective and had taken twenty prisoners from an anti-aircraft unit who said that they had only arrived on the previous night. " A " and " B " Companies quickly took their objectives, and it was clear that the first part of the operation was going well against a dispirited resistance. The Commandos were progressing equally well in the Lauenberg area, and, in fact, captured the bridge over the Elbe-Trave Canal intact at about 0630 hours. By 0700 hours the whole operation was over, and the Schnakenbek garrison of dejected Green Police were on their way to the crossing place en route for captivity.

Although the infantry had got over unscathed, and, with the exception of Tactical Headquarters, whose arrival coincided with the arrival of thirty or forty shells, unshaken, the shelling of the crossing was becoming more intense, and the vehicle party had an exceedingly uncomfortable time until they got clear of the quarry. After this, shelling ceased in the afternoon, the crossing was severely harrassed by air attack so that " C " Squadron of the Reconnaissance Regiment was non-operational on arrival having had fourteen vehicles put out of action. It was only through the devoted skill of Sergeant W. Murdoch, of Jedburgh, the Transport Sergeant, that all our vehicles reached the Battalion unharmed. He remained in the quarry all day, under continuous shelling or bombing, and with great ability organised the clearing of the landing site. For this gallantry he was awarded the Military Medal.

By the middle of the day it was obvious that there was no depth to the enemy's positions, neither was there any sign of a counter attack from Schwarzenbek. 46 Brigade and 227 Brigade were expanding the bridgehead on the right and left respectively. and vigorous carrier patrols of the 8th Royal Scots found only wounded Germans in Krukow and none in Juliusberg. The K.O.S.B. and the Royal Scots Fusiliers were originally to have occupied these two places preparatory to pushing on at first light. The Brigade Commander, however, now ordered the Battalion to move up to Krukow and remain there with the Royal Scots and go on to Gulzow in the morning. But Major Jackson preferred to go straight through to Gulzow, particularly as an Officer of the Special Air Service had reported to us that he had already been to look at Gulzow and had only found a few recalcitrant civilians. Permission for this plan was readily granted, and by 2300 hours the Battalion was firmly established there. By this time the civilians had lost any recalcitrance they had and were cowering in their cellars, while several fires raged in the village.

During the previous morning the enemy laid some very heavy artillery fire on the area of the crossing, most of which was fortunately ineffective as it fell on the top of the cliff; though one never knew when a salvo would clear the cliff and land exactly on the crossing point. Some did, and some fell in the river. Apart from this vicious shelling, which was continuous, there was a single heavy gun, sited near Gulzow, which fired regularly every minute throughout the morning. At about mid-day shelling ceased until the evening, just as the Battalion was moving off to Krukow, and then between forty and fifty rounds were fired over our heads to land near the river —and not a single one exploded. It was though an unwilling gun team, ordered to make a last effort, had deliberately omitted to fuse the shells. At any rate the incident gave the impression that the end was imminent.

CHAPTER XVI.

THE END.

ONE of the most remarkable features of the campaign through France and Germany was the facility with which the enemy had given up the major water barriers in the line of advance of the British army, and here was the widest of them all, crossed with practically no ground opposition, no casualties to the Battalion, and an advance of five miles beyond the river made on the same day. The war had really become a "phoney war." More so, indeed, when at eleven o'clock the next morning the Reconnaissance Regiment reported that prisoners said that all tanks and self-propelled guns in the area had been ordered to withdraw to Hamburg and all infantry to Lubeck. They also reported that one of their officers was negotiating for the surrender of eighteen hundred troops in the area. The troops were a motley crowd but were commanded by S.S. officers. On the left, in 227 Brigade sector, a similar incident was taking place, this time in connection with the evacuation of what was alleged to be a poison gas store near Geestacht. In the first case the enemy surrendered, in the second they agreed to withdraw to an appointed line.

At this stage the General proposed to put the 6th K.O.S.B. under command of 227 Brigade and push us into the Geestach area, and Major Jackson went to 227 Brigade Headquarters for orders from the General. Having heard, however, that the gas dump was really a dump of propellant mixture for V2's, and that one shell or bomb in the middle of it would probably kill everyone for ten miles around, Major Jackson did not relish the prospect, in spite of the fact that the German commander of the dump had been carefully kept at his post. He diplomatically persuaded General Barber that it would be unfortunate and complicated for the 6th K.O.S.B. to be side-tracked into the 227th Brigade area, while one of their Battalions would almost certainly be used on the 44th Brigade axis. And so the plan was changed.

The 6th K.O.S.B. were now to go on to Kollow and then to Brunstorf on the edge of the great Sachsenwald, where the Reconnaissance Regiment found the enemy hitting back hard with infantry and self-propelled guns. On the 30th April the Battalion moved to Kollow and patrolled with carriers part of the Gulzower Holz. They captured some prisoners, one of whom had been with a party of thirty pioneers sent to destroy the bridges at Gulzow, but they arrived too late, and the other twenty-nine decided to retire. The Carrier Platoon also found three big guns of approximately twelve inch calibre with their pieces destroyed. They were presumably the heavy guns which had been firing so regularly the day before. By a sad mischance, the leading "wasp" carrier, having reached the limit of the patrol, was turning round to return, when it touched a Teller mine and "brewed up," severely burning the driver, Private Miller.

On the following day we took a sweep round westwards through Hamwarde and Worth to attack Brunstorf. After the comparative quiet of the past two days, Brunstorf gave promise of being a fairly tough proposition, particularly as the German artillery seemed to have got trails down again. But after a short exchange of fire about a hundred Germans gave themselves up, while the rest retired into the Sachsenwald. A patrol found the enemy still active at a position on the edge of the wood, and there remained the possibility of a counter attack. Nothing, however, materialised except some mortaring. What remained of the enemy was cleared up during the next day when 44 Brigade swept the Sachsenwald north of the railway from east to west, while 46 Brigade swept the southern part. At one stage of the proceedings the Battalion was almost welcomed by a party of German girls standing outside a house on the railway line. This was too suspicious for Private Errington and Corporal McCormick who were well trained in security matters. They answered the welcome by promptly searching the house and emerging triumphantly with half a dozen soldiers who were hiding there.

One of the tasks of the Battalion was to seize the Schloss at Friedrichsruhe, where it was thought that Himmler might be, or might have had his headquarters recently. No trace was found of Himmler, however, but Major Twogood did find Prince Bismark telephoning the situation to Hamburg. In the Schloss he also found the Swiss and Swedish Consulates from Hamburg, and the building was therefore immediately given neutral status. But although all resistance seemed at an end, there were still odd groups in the woods who were prepared to fire their ammunition before finally giving up. It was at the hands of one such group of Arbeits Dienst that we had our last casualty.

The plan was for the whole Battalion to concentrate for the night in the village after the woods had been cleared and 46 Brigade had finished their task. They were behind in time and an unfortunate incident nearly occurred when, in the evening, Major Jackson set out in his carrier to look for "A" Company, and, losing his way in the maze of rides and tracks, entered Aumuhle from the rear while fighting was still in progress in front of it.

By this time negotiations were in progress for the surrender of Hamburg, and a very large area north-east of the city was declared neutral. The war had suddenly become an exercise, and the umpires had declared a truce in which to make certain redispositions. The next two moves, first to Kronshorst, and then to Dellingsdorf, were " soft hat " moves through this neutral zone—a curious anti-climax. The scene at Dellingsdorf was indeed remarkable. Situated almost midway between Lubeck and Hamburg on what was the main road before the autobahn was built, we witnessed a most interesting stream of traffic, most of which was going towards Hamburg. Streams of dirty, dejected soldiers poured along the road to be diverted into the Battalion cage for onward transmission. Some protested at being made prisoners as they had discharge papers signed on the previous day, and said that at Lubeck they had been told that the war was over and that they could go home! Now a group of farm carts taking what remained of a troop of artillery; now a broken bus filled with once arrogant Luftwaffe men; now a motor-cyclist solemnly taking a convoy of signal equipment probably containing much secret and costly material, to report to a British unit, carrying as his authority a hastily written pencil note from an armoured unit; all variety of men and vehicles passed along that road, side by side with hundreds of displaced persons who, but a few hours ago, had been the slave workers of the Germans. The powerful, well-disciplined Wehrmacht was nothing but a miserable, dirty, disillusioned rabble, the living example to all the villagers of the penalty of over-weaning ambition—defeat!

The war was indeed over for them, but not yet for us, and there was still a formation of S.S. troops making a last stand in the Forst Segeberg. A two-sided exercise with troops was later arranged between a Wehrmacht division and these S.S. troops with the armoured cars of the 15th Reconnaissance Regiment picketting the battle area. The result was that, after a bombardment and an attack by the Wehrmacht, the S.S. surrendered.

It was while the Colonel, who had returned the previous day, was having dinner with the Officers of Battalion Headquarters, that the Mess Corporal, Corporal Poxton, with his usual politeness and restraint, quietly entered the room and said, " Excuse me, sir, but the Signaller on the Brigade set has just said that one of the Signallers at Brigade has told him that hostilities will cease tomorrow morning." This was immediately confirmed, and later in the night the official message was received, " Germans surrendered unconditionally 1840 hours 4 May 1945. Hostilities on all Second fronts will cease at 0800 hours 5 May 1945." So the order, awaited for all those years, had come at last—with no more ceremony or apparent stir than an allotment of the Mobile Bath Unit.

EPILOGUE.

By the time that this book is published, the 6th Border Battalion will have finished its work and have ceased to exist. As the duplicate of the 4th Battalion, it was a second line Territorial Unit drawn almost entirely from Berwickshire, Roxburghshire and Selkirkshire. Only a few of those Borderers who joined the Battalion in 1939 remained with it to see the end of the war; few indeed of those who landed with it in Normandy remained. Fifty-five Officers and one thousand and ninety men became casualties during the campaign. Some indication may be got from these figures of the part played by the Battalion since the invasion, and from the fact that the Battalion received more awards than any other unit in the 15th Scottish Division. It is always but a very small proportion of a unit which receives such honours, hundreds earn them by their bravery. To mention all those men who have deserved such honours is impossible, and so they remain unsung. But although the world does not know of their deeds, these men are honoured in the hearts and memories of their comrades, and they themselves can say,

"We have triumphed : this achievement turns the bane to antidote, unsuccesses to success,

Many thought-worn eves and morrows to a morrow free of thought."

APPENDIX "A."

HONOURS and AWARDS, 6th K.O.S.B.
(Complete to 4th February, 1946).

D.S.O.
Lieutenant-Colonel J. G. Shillington.
Lieutenant-Colonel C. W. P. Richardson.

Bar to D.S.O.
Lieutenant-Colonel C. W. P. Richardson.

M.C.
Captain J. Elliot.
Captain N. C. Rollo.
Captain G. E. R. Carey.
Captain R. H. McDonald.
Major J. D. Henson.
Lieutenant J. Woods.
Major J. M. Tinniswood.
Lieutenant J. W. Fullarton.
Lieutenant I. M. McDonald.
Captain J. R. P. Baggaley.
Major M. W. Twogood.
3186162 Company Sergeant-Major A. Millar, M.M.
3181504 Regimental Sergeant-Major. J. Walls.

D.C.M.
3194543 Lance-Sergeant W. Thomson.
3189201 Sergeant J. A. Telfer.
14424561 Lance-Corporal A. Beck.

M.M.
3186825 Company Sergeant-Major P. Telford.
3186821 Company Sergeant-Major A. Millar.
3187557 Lance-Corporal J. Ord.
3190681 Lance-Sergeant W. Shiel.
6977405 Private T. Dawson.
2927383 Corporal A. Bain.
3187057 Lance-Sergeant G. I. Campbell.

Honours and Awards

M.M.—*continued*
 4969974 Sergeant H. Taylor.
 3188068 Private H. Lindie.
 5114968 Sergeant C. G. Lee.
 3190019 Sergeant J. McLaren.
 6978089 Sergeant C. O'Neal.
 3192238 Lance-Sergeant R. White.
 3195405 Sergeant W. Murdoch.
 3602585 Lance-Corporal J. Brooks.
 3190678 Sergeant C. E. Thomson.

Bar to M.M.
 3187057 Sergeant G. I. Campbell.

Mentions in Despatches.
 Rev. A. W. Sawyer.
 Captain R. M. Woollcombe.
 Captain A. H. Elder.
 Captain F. E. Burnett.
 Lieutenant (Quartermaster) J. W. A. Smith.
 Lieutenant G. W. Parmley.
 3185339 Company Sergeant-Major J. Lyall.
 6138717 Company Sergeant-Major R. Overington.
 2819698 Sergeant W. Murdoch.
 3193362 Lance-Sergeant D. Hunt.
 3194543 Lance-Sergeant W. Thomson.
 3187511 Lance-Corporal J. Keats.
 14651208 Lance-Corporal G. Vye.
 6411762 Lance-Corporal R. Stepton-Allan.
 14211627 Private S. Gibson.
 3194421 Private J. Milne.
 3193177 Private G. Price.
 3190603 Private J. Cleaver.

Croix de Guerre.
 Captain J. Moffat (with Gilt Star).
 3191945 Private J. Tracey (with Bronze Star).

American Bronze Star.
 5050612 Sergeant W. Twigg.

1946

Martin's Printing Works Ltd.
64-66 West Street
BERWICK-ON-TWEED